Why me?

Children talking to ChildLine about bullying

A ChildLine study

Written by Mary MacLeod and Sally Morris

Foreword by Valerie Howarth

Publication sponsored by:
Barclays Bank
The Mercers Company
The Reader's Digest Trust
The Sandra Trust

Contents

List of Tables

About ChildLine

ChildLine was established in 1986 to listen to, comfort and protect children in trouble or danger. By 31st March 1995, the agency had counselled 473,048 children. All calls are free to the children - they are paid for by ChildLine.

The Charity's first objective is to answer every child's call. We have managed to answer more and more calls every year since the service was opened, and currently answer around 3,200 every day from our five centres across the U.K.[1] Despite this, we know from British Telecom monitoring of our lines that many more children try to reach our counsellors, but cannot get through, because all lines are busy. Only with more funding will ChildLine be able to close the gap between the demand and our ability to respond.

ChildLine was originally conceived as a bridging service between children who were being abused and sources of help. But children themselves, calling in their tens of thousands, have defined the service they want. Some ring us once because of a crisis in their lives. They may be pregnant; they have been physically or sexually assaulted; they have suffered bereavement. Others call because they want to talk over some aspects of growing up - friendship, falling in love, sexuality, school problems. Some ring about chronic difficulties which persistently trouble them: bullying, loneliness or depression, domestic violence in their homes. Sometimes children call because they have no one else to talk to. In 1994-95 alone, over 90,000 children were counselled about these and other problems and concerns.

Our counsellors aim to listen attentively to what children say; children are encouraged to consider carefully the consequences of taking particular courses of action as they discuss with counsellors how to proceed. We try, wherever appropriate, to help them identify an adult they know and trust, in whom they can confide their problems and concerns.

---

[1] ChildLine bases are located in:

HQ – London	Scotland – Glasgow
Midlands – Nottingham	North West – Manchester	Wales/Cymru – Swansea and Rhyl.

As funding permits, five further centres are planned to cover the rest of the United Kingdom.

Many young people find it difficult to talk about what is worrying them straightaway, and use various means of testing the service before they feel confident enough to speak to a counsellor. Children seldom want ChildLine to rush into action; usually they will carefully guard their anonymity, and want to be in control of the counselling and referral process, if the latter is to be instituted. Very early in ChildLine's history, our counsellors learnt that attempting to intervene before a child is ready simply results in forfeiting the trust of the child, who may then never call back. So, except in situations where the child is judged to be in extreme danger, ChildLine's service is child-led and confidential to the caller.

From its beginnings, the heart of ChildLine has been its volunteer counsellors, who now number over 700. They are of all ages and from all walks of life. Volunteers receive thorough initial and ongoing training, and constant support and supervision, to enable them to offer the children a service they can trust.

ChildLine is also committed to ensuring that children's voices are more widely heard, as a means of promoting changes in social policy, practice and provision relating to children. We achieve this through the powerful evidence of the children themselves, taken directly from their calls to ChildLine. This report on bullying is one example of this commitment. Among others have been the published reports on ChildLine's previous special lines, such as the Bullying Line (1991), Boarding School Line (1992) and ChildLine for Children in Care (1994).

Author's note

Throughout this report, the terms 'children' and 'young people' are used, interchangeably, to indicate children up to the age of 18.

Finally, in accordance with ChildLine's policy of confidentiality, names and other details of individual children quoted have been altered in order that they cannot be identified.

Acknowledgements

This study by ChildLine of children's experiences of bullying was written by Mary MacLeod and Sally Morris, with research assistance from Helen Wheatley and Jenny Seale. It includes significant contributions from Hereward Harrison and Barbara Lees, and a foreword by Valerie Howarth.

Particular thanks are due to all the ChildLine counsellors who talk to children with such attention and kindness. Their experience and expertise has contributed to the approach to helping children and young people which is promoted in this book. Within our counselling operation, the helpline was the particular responsibility of Lingam Moodley, Patricia Walker, Louise Roscoe, John Flynn and Veronica O'Hare.

No ChildLine research or campaigning work could take place without the dedication of the ChildLine press office and the administrative staff, who key in data from records, run rotas, and ensure the smooth running of the service. Special thanks go to Wendy Toms, Natasha Finlayson, Gill Sanders, Bernie Burrell, Jenny Seale, Tricia Lester and Sonia Tavares.

This project was a partnership between the BBC and ChildLine. It was Chris Longley, Executive Editor Social Action who first approached us and Kathryn Morrison who co-ordinated production across BBC Radio and Television. It was their efforts that ensured so many children and adults concerned about bullying were reached through extensive and wide ranging BBC programme coverage and print material which they produced and helped disseminate. Thanks are also due to the then Controller of Radio 5, Pat Ewing, the many radio and television producers involved as well as Helen Wheeler, Penny Luker-Brown and Emma Woodrow.

The project and research were made possible by generous donations from a variety of organisations, trusts and corporate donors:

Barclays Bank
Baring Foundation
BBC Children in Need
BT
The Calouste Gulbenkian Foundation
The Corporation of London
Department for Education
The Mercers Company
The Prince's Trust
The Reader's Digest Trust
The Sandra Trust
Woolworths plc
Whitbread Charitable Trust
Mizz magazine
MG magazine
ACE (Advisory Centre for Education)

The research publication was sponsored by:

Barclays Bank
The Mercers Company
The Readers Digest Trust
The Sandra Trust

The typescript was painstakingly produced by Angela Packer, whose charm never deserted her, however many changes were made.

Thanks to Sophie Epstein (11) for the title.

Above all, we wish to thank the children who talked to ChildLine, the schools who participated in the study, and the teachers, parents and young people who completed questionnaires and were prepared to be interviewed for this study. This book is dedicated to them.

Any errors which may be found are, of course, the responsibility of the authors.

Foreword
by Valerie Howarth

There can be no doubt now - after all the work undertaken on bullying - that it is a widespread and perpetual problem which cannot be totally eliminated. This is not an excuse for doing nothing. Simply, if adults fail to understand the nature of bullying - that we are dealing with something which is ongoing and will be with each new generation of children - we can lose the energy and will to keep working at it.

This ChildLine study - with its window into children's lives and feelings - demonstrates conclusively that children and young people want and need adults to keep working at it. There are groups of children who are especially vulnerable; those who are isolated or targeted because of disability or difference, and those living away from home. Specific points in school life are dangerous - transitions from one school or class to another and the incorporation of new students into an already formed class.

But this report shows that any child may become a target and, if our case study in schools is representative, that most already have. For some, this is a brief period of fear, exclusion or humiliation, which may nevertheless leave emotional scars. Others are entrapped in a relentless campaign of harassment and violence and can come to believe that suicide is the only way out.

Many adults can remember only too well what it is like to be a child and to be bullied. For those who cannot remember, it is worth imagining what it might feel like to come into work one day and have no-one speak to you or reply to anything you say - and to have to go in there every day as this goes on and on. Few can withstand such rejection.

This report also shows that bullying happens in the context of children growing-up and learning how to get on with each other. In this sense, there is an inevitability about it. So schools should not be ashamed to admit that bullying happens in their backyard. It happens in all schools and institutions, and according to the secondary school children surveyed here, mainly in classrooms.

What this report calls for is an end to the reluctance to pursue the tried and tested programmes of action to reduce the incidence and seriousness of bullying. It is time for a strategy in each school and institution - and one that relies on words and action.

These programmes not only safeguard children from harm, they help in every aspect of children's development - intellectual, social and moral. What could be more important than strengthening children's sense of, and respect for fairness and justice? The programmes do not rely on punishment, but on a wide range of responses to individual and group behaviour, for which children can themselves take responsibility. Children are a real but underused resource in tackling bullying.

But they cannot manage without adult will and commitment. It has to be acknowledged that adults can find that the frequency of children's complaints of bullying reduces the impact on them of children's actual feelings. Bullying complaints become commonplace and boring. If this can be resisted, adult vigilance can make all the difference between happiness and misery for children in their care. ChildLine hopes that this book will be an inspiration for parents, carers and teachers to listen to each child's account of being bullied as if it was the first - and then, together with the child, to do something about it.

Valerie Howarth
Executive Director
ChildLine

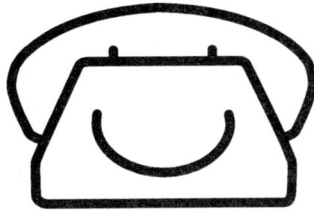

Chapter 1

Introduction

"I can't imagine not being frightened."

Ever since its launch in October 1986, ChildLine has heard from children about bullying. If we were ever tempted to dismiss bullying as just one of the hazards of childhood which children ought to buck up and learn how to cope with; if we had ever thought that it 'makes a man of you', we certainly could not have kept these beliefs beyond the first few calls. For bullying causes real suffering and if adults don't know this, children and young people do. And, given the means to say what they are going through, they can. Since ChildLine began in October 1986, over 60,000 children have been counselled about bullying.

This book aims to bring together what children and adults have told ChildLine about bullying and how to help. It draws on conversations with children over nine years, and on the research study undertaken as part of the joint ChildLine/BBC Social Action project on bullying, which ran from March to October in 1994, counselling 4494 children on a special helpline.

While the Bullying Line was in progress, the story broke of yet another child affected by bullying who had killed herself. It was clear from this child's diary that she had thought of ringing ChildLine. We do not know whether she did. In those tragic cases it is not possible to know all the factors which lead a child to death and not right to ascribe blame too readily. But it echoed for us the words of many children we have talked to:

"I don't think I can go on any more."

"I wish I could go to sleep and never wake up..."

"I would like to end it all...I can't take any more of this..."

"Suicide would be better than going to school again."

These voices tell us that bullying is very bad for children and some are driven by it to the depths of despair. In the research sample of 1500 child callers studied here, more than 60 had contemplated or attempted suicide. This was four per cent of the sample and we have every reason to think this figure applies across all the children who talk to us about bullying.

It is universally accepted by educationalists that being bullied can interfere with children's mental health and their educational development. But it is clear from research that even when they have not had direct experience of being bullied, children, having seen it and seen the effect it has, fear it (NSPCC 1995).

For those bullied in public or institutional care, the situation is very bleak. Our Time to listen (1994) study of children in care and our previous bullying report, Bullying: the Child's View (1991), showed that to be unable to get away from the bullying at night is misery indeed. Children can feel driven into solutions which expose them to even more difficulty or danger, like feigning illness, fighting back, truanting from school, running away and trying to kill themselves.

A 14-year-old girl rang from boarding school about her friend's plight. Her friend had already phoned ChildLine about persistent psychological bullying from a group of girls. "It is horrible to be hit but I think mental bullying is worse," she said. With encouragement from ChildLine she had decided to approach her form teacher and this had worked for a brief time but now the bullying was worse and she was in despair, not eating and suffering nightmares.

Her friend was very worried that she might try to kill herself.

Both of these girls found it very difficult to contemplate approaching their parents for help, though, eventually, having talked everything through, the caller decided she had to speak to her mother in order to get help to her friend before she did something disastrous.

One of the privileges of talking to children about their troubles is receiving the child's eye view of the adult world. However, it can then be extremely hard to keep patience with the difficulties adults (teachers, parents, police and adult bystanders to street bullying) have in acting to keep children safe.

"Dear ChildLine, I would like a lot of advice because I get bullied severely. I have to put up with black eyes, sprained ankles, kicked shins and many more attacks. I really want advice because it happens every day in school and out. I feel nobody likes me except my family and friends. I am 10 years old and I get badly bullied. I hope to be hearing from you soon.

Simon

P.S. The headteacher is scared of the bully's parents so he does nothing about it."

This was one of the letters about bullying ChildLine received during the bullying project. Simon's 'diagnosis' of his headteacher's problem may appear overblown and childish. Yet a similar perception emerged in a lengthy letter from the grandfather of a six-year-old girl describing his and his daughter's many attempts to get the headteacher of an infant school to protect the child from bullying by an older boy in the school. Though initially supportive, the head teacher had become very dismissive of their child's plight because, in their view, he was being intimidated by the parents of the bullying child, and taking the easier road.

Article 19 of the United Nations Convention on the Rights of the

Child requires that children should be kept safe from harm, an aim which is easy to agree but not so easy to achieve. The very fact that bullying is so prevalent, according to Whitney and Smith (1993), one in four primary school age children and one in ten secondary school children suffering incidents each term, can lead to a sense of helplessness, hopelessness or even boredom in adults charged with the responsibility to care for and protect children. There is unlikely to be a teacher who has not groaned privately when bullying comes up.

Yet each generation of school children needs the same attentiveness to their well-being and social development as those preceding them. So schools should perceive their anti-bullying programme in the same way as they do the National Curriculum, as something which is delivered to each cohort of children with the same enthusiasm, quality and care. However tiring it is for adults to continue having to deal with the same intractable problems, we have to persist.

History of ChildLine's work on bullying

The present study is ChildLine's second major project on bullying. What we have learned from children during the project makes it unlikely to be the last.

ChildLine's first anti-bullying project was established in 1991, thanks to funding from the Calouste Gulbenkian Foundation which must be commended for its consistent support of projects aimed at reducing bullying in schools. A special bullying line was set up which enabled us to:

- reach more of the children who needed to talk to us;
- publicly indicate to children that they could ring ChildLine about bullying - and the increase in the number of calls about bullying afterwards received by the main ChildLine service demonstrated that this message to children did get through;
- report on what children could tell us about bullying to help change adult responses to children's complaints.

It was clear from our first study (La Fontaine 1991) that children and adults have very different conceptions of bullying. Since they define it differently, it is not surprising that they have differing expectations and views about how it should be dealt with.

The study also revealed that much more bullying happens in groups than had been previously identified. Therefore, understanding the way children's groups organise themselves is crucially important if bullying is to be successfully tackled. Contrary to the assumption that children are best left to sort it out for themselves, the study also confirmed that **children do need and want adult intervention to stop bullying.**

Since then, knowledge about bullying has increased; many excellent books and pamphlets have been published to assist adults tackling bullying in schools and elsewhere (see bibliography); and much innovative project work has been undertaken in schools. Some poignantly tragic deaths and terrifyingly violent bullying incidents have drawn attention to the extremes of violence and distress which are part of the spectrum of bullying behaviour. So bullying has become more 'on the agenda'. But it has not been clear how much, if anything, has changed for children. This was the context for ChildLine's second anti-bullying project.

The Bullying Project 1994

BBC Social Action approached ChildLine to set up a joint bullying project which was to have four components:
- a special helpline;
- extensive media coverage of the issue of bullying - to increase public awareness of children's experience of bullying and to spread information about how bullying can be tackled;
- printed materials for parents, teachers and young people - to assist in tackling bullying;
- a study of callers' current experience of bullying - to expand and up-date our knowledge of bullying from the child's point of view.

The helpline was launched on 5th March 1994 by BBC TV's *That's Life* and BBC Radio 5 alongside the BBC Social Action project on bullying. The helpline ended over seven months later on 14th October 1994. The BBC and ChildLine obtained funding from Barclays Bank Community Enterprise, the Baring Foundation, BBC Children in Need, BT, The Calouste Gulbenkian Foundation, the Corporation of London, Department for Education, The Mercers Company, The Prince's Trust, The Reader's Digest Trust, The Sandra Trust, Woolworths plc, and the Whitbread Charitable Trust. *Mizz* and *MG* magazines produced the print materials for children, and the Advisory Centre for Education (ACE) Ltd and Sonia Sharp those for parents and teachers.

The press and media coverage was very extensive, ensuring that advice on how to help bullied children was widely disseminated, even if all the children in need of help could not be reached by the resources of the helpline.

From the first day of the helpline to its last, ChildLine was deluged with calls, by its end answering over 58,530 calls. While we do not know how many children these call figures represent, we can say with certainty that the demand was substantial and it tells us that we cannot be complacent about or dismissive of bullying despite all the recent efforts.

Counselling children on the Bullying Line

While the helpline was in progress, we counselled 4494 children on bullying: 3704 girls and 790 boys. Some children called only once, others called back for ongoing help.

ChildLine views child callers as children asking for help, not necessarily making an allegation or a complaint - though that might be an outcome. ChildLine works with children towards a solution they consider helpful, and will mediate, on children's behalf between them and responsible adults if the children wish, also giving information about how to approach the adults in their lives about their difficulties. Children phone ChildLine not only because they need help but also because in doing so they do not lose control of their own lives. (Their desire for some control also emerges powerfully from the present study.)

During the conversation we assist and encourage the children to view themselves as persons with the right to be treated fairly and to be afforded protection from injury or abuse. In offering help we have three aims:

- to give children the relief and comfort of telling what has been happening and how they feel;
- to help them plan how to end the bullying;
- to begin the process of undoing the harm done to their confidence and development.

Children calling the Bullying Line had usually already taken some steps themselves to stop being bullied. We began by acknowledging this and praising them for their efforts and their courage. Where we went from there depended on the child's individual situation and the network of help they could call upon.

Children talked to us about many troubles they had alongside bullying: family relationship problems, problems with friends and sexual and physical abuse were the most common. And these were attended to in the counselling exchange. While it is commonplace to ascribe being a victim of bullying to other difficulties children have in their lives, the overall picture was not one of troubled child victims seeking out bullies; rather the reverse, of children completely confounded by finding themselves the object of so much hate, ridicule and violence, desperately trying to figure out why, and becoming, in consequence, deeply troubled. Again and again children said to us: why me?

Calls from adults

"I don't want to make a fuss."

Nearly 700 parents called the Bullying Line. Most had made serious but unsuccessful attempts to get the school to tackle the bullying their child complained of. They were calling in absolute frustration. Parents often described being brushed off, feeling bullied or intimidated.

One mother called about her 16-year-old severely disabled son who had, in a previous school, been subjected to gross bullying and physical abuse by a teacher. The boy could not talk and so it was only his increasing distress, and evidence from other children, that alerted the mother to the bullying.

This mother summoned her courage and went to the Head who was dismayed to hear about the extent and seriousness of the bullying and promised to make sure it stopped. Apparently it did stop briefly but resumed. The teacher concerned is still working at the school despite the mother's complaints. She feels in an absolute quandary because she thinks other children may be at risk and she feels very guilty about her failure, as she sees it, to protect her vulnerable son; but her husband does not wish her to do anything more about it because of the 'fuss' it would involve.

There were some desperate accounts of parents dealing with extremely distressed, sometimes suicidal children, having to force unwilling children to school, taking children out of school to be educated at home, and getting into very combative stances with schools and governors to try to get their children protected. A few were considering legal action. Many were considering moving children to another school, often against the advice of the school or education authority. Some had already moved their children.

Researching bullying

It is one of ChildLine's aims to ensure that what children say is brought to public attention on their behalf. While this is imperative for all children, it is especially important for children living away from home in care and boarding school, and for those whose communication difficulties render them even less able to say they are being bullied.

BBC Social Action, ChildLine's partner in the project, ensured it was highly publicised at the time by the BBC, and other media soon took up the story. The project's printed materials allowed ChildLine and the BBC to promote awareness of children's experience of bullying to children, parents and teachers. The research study was established to ensure that our reading of children's experiences is organised, up to date, and systematic, not merely impressionistic.

There were two elements to the research reported here:

- an analysis of a sample of calls to the Bullying Line;
- a case study of four schools, comprising questionnaires and interviews.

The primary purpose of the Line was of course to counsel children and the counselling approach was child-centred. This confined the areas of exploration to those helpful to the individual child in the counselling process. As soon as each call was finished, counsellors wrote up a record for counselling purposes but also for research. While conversations with children are not conducted in order to get specific information from them, they tell us a great deal about themselves and their problems. Though information is patchy in some areas and the level of 'no data' responses is high, the detailed analysis of these calls provides a unique account of children's experience.

However, by its nature, ChildLine hears from children about problems, and the picture emerging from their calls may not represent the general experience of children. In order to broaden the base of information and to give a more rounded picture of children's experience of bullying in schools, we undertook the case study in four schools. The study involved discussion of their anti-bullying strategies, questionnaire surveys of children, parents and staff, followed by in-depth, structured interviews with a sample of just over 100 children who responded to the questionnaire.

Though the research had two discrete parts, which are described in detail in chapters 2 and 3, the findings of the research are described and discussed together, with evidence drawn freely from both the helpline and the schools.

Main findings

The present study reveals that the types of behaviour described as bullying, where it takes place and the effects on children involved, are similar to those recorded in the ChildLine 1991 study and others. Yet some distinctions are notable.

More bullying incidents were reported to be taking place outside school environments. This tallies with public perceptions that the streets and playgrounds have become more violent places for children and with recent horrific cases of violence outside school premises. Though our sample is too small and our helpline research base too particular for us to make definitive statements about this, we think the evidence strongly suggests that urgent attention ought to be paid to making the streets safer for children.

Similarly, the level of violent incidents reported appears to have increased since our last study. Though we cannot draw definite conclusions about a general increase in violent bullying, this is, nevertheless, very troubling.

It is also disappointing to find that, despite the higher profile bullying has had, the increase and availability of materials for use in schools, and the numerous anti-bullying campaigns and projects, the incidence of bullying reported by children in the school survey is very high - higher than that of other surveys. Since incidence rates link to the definition of bullying, this may mean that children are more able or willing to name their experience as bullying. Sceptics may suggest that children are now calling any tiff bullying, but the study suggests that children are sophisticated in the nuances of social interactions. As one 12-year-old girl put it about name-calling: **"Sometimes it's joking, but when it's serious, they do it with their voice. It's like more steady and loud and serious."**

Perhaps most disappointing is the finding that a great deal of bullying takes place **inside** classrooms. Secondary school children describe it as the place they are most likely to be bullied. This does suggest a level of adult tolerance of bullying which is disquieting and unacceptable.

The major positive change revealed by the study is that many more children now feel able to tell about being bullied. While this is heartening, it suggests that the emphasis of some of the anti-bullying work is misplaced. A great deal of it derives from the premise that children find it hard to tell, and the emphasis has been on school strategies which promote telling; for example the Department for Education pack is entitled: *Bullying: Don't Suffer in Silence.*

While telling is a first step, it is not nearly enough and cannot be the sole focus of school programmes. Most of the children we talked to, like Simon quoted earlier, had told. For them, the problem was not reluctance to tell but the reluctance of adults to act or act effectively.

They bitterly complained about adults who advised them to ignore it and it would stop. They cannot ignore it and adults should stop telling them to do so. We heard from both children and parents who were in despair because they felt they had done everything they could do and the bullying still continued.

The overwhelming majority (97%) of children calling the Bullying Line who had told teachers or staff were calling because the bullying was still going on. They reported being met with various responses when they told: 31 per cent of children reported that telling had resulted in no action; 13 per cent were advised to ignore it; six per cent were not believed; three per cent were told 'there is no bullying here'; but 39 per cent reported action being taken, and eight per cent that the bullies were excluded. In all, 53 per cent of 'complaints' led to no action and 47 per cent to action. In either case the bullying continued.

So though it is true that some children still find it hard to say they are being bullied and so cannot get help, a significant number of children who do tell and ask for help commonly find that help is not forthcoming or not effective.

The other major finding from this study is information on how children themselves understand bullying - from the point of view of those bullied, bullying and bystanding. Only one per cent of the children counselled on the lines said they were 'bullies'; but a sizeable proportion of the children surveyed in the schools admitted to bullying behaviour. This, alongside information provided by bullied children about who bullied them and why, and those child callers who were worried about other children being bullied, has helped to produce a clearer and less simplistic picture of why and how children bully.

They describe a complex pattern of escalating difficulties which takes time and commitment from child, parents, friends and teachers to unravel. This is something understood by children themselves. Indirect and verbal forms of bullying, disturbing in themselves, can quickly deteriorate into physically threatening behaviour. Therefore all bullying should be taken seriously. Because the pattern is complex, there is no quick and easy solution schools can apply to stop or reduce bullying behaviour; rather they need to put in place a wide-ranging approach, flexible enough to respond to the variety of bullying incidents encountered. However, our study shows little evidence that the enormous range and richness of guidance for teachers and schools is being routinely used to reduce bullying. Those children calling the Bullying Line from care or boarding school presented a picture of acute distress. Surely their particular vulnerability requires constant staff attention to the prevention of bullying. ChildLine thinks the time has come for direction not guidance.

Children in this study give a clear message that the most effective way to resolve bullying incidents must involve the children themselves in clarifying the exact nature of the problem and planning what should best be done. The involvement of parents, teachers and school governors in implementing a school's anti-bullying policy strengthens the anti-bullying culture within the school, and is essential in providing invaluable support to the individual children concerned. But the enterprise cannot succeed unless children are centrally involved.

The case study undertaken in schools is suggestive rather than definitive because only four schools were studied. But interesting possibilities emerged from it. Promoting a culture of 'decency' within a school seems to be the bedrock on which real success depends. Organisational cultures are complex, and changing a developed culture can be difficult, especially if intimidation ensures compliance with cultural norms. The role of the headteacher in this process appears to be pivotal.

Though ChildLine usually hears the bad news rather than the good, we did have some calls from children wanting to record what made a difference and the headteacher's attitude is seen as making a great difference.

A 13-year-old boy caller told us of a year of misery at a school where his and also his parents' attempts to get the problem tackled had had no effect. His parents had finally decided to move the boy to another school which had worked out very well because, the boy reported, the headteacher was very clear that bullying was out of order and everyone knew this.

It is unlikely that a culture of 'decency' can prevail if the headteacher's behaviour and that of his or her staff does not model what they expect of children. The school study, limited though it was, bears out the Elton Inquiry's view that schools which rely too heavily on punishment to deter bad behaviour "are likely to be disappointed" (HMSO, 1989). Though schools will always have to have clear guidance and sanctions on what is acceptable and unacceptable behaviour, they also have to find ways of helping children to develop skills in diffusing conflict and managing their feelings.

If the majority of bullying behaviour is viewed as a likely and predictable expression of children's struggle to manage being together in groups, exacerbated by lack of supervision and inaction, then such an understanding demands a non-punitive strategy towards much of the bullying alongside a tariff of sanctions for 'anti-social' acts. This allows bullying behaviour to be tackled in a number of ways - through curriculum work, groupwork, mediation and peer counselling as well as individual responses - without making things worse for the children complaining and the children involved in bullying.

Complaining

When help fails, it is important that children and parents have ways of saying so. Most children and parents who call ChildLine have no idea how to follow-up an approach to teachers which fails to deal with the problem. They either feel fearful of talking to people in authority or they are worried about the consequences for their children of making a complaint. They are easily intimidated. Those who do feel able to pursue a complaint find real obstacles in the way. It appears from what children say that almost everyone gets bored or exasperated with the problem if it is not solved easily and at once.

This is why, as part of our bullying project last year, ChildLine lobbied for the Parent's Charter to include specific information on bullying and a guarantee that complaints of bullying would be taken seriously, and provided evidence to the Citizen's Charter Complaints Task Force on children's and parents' experience of complaining about bullying in schools. In our view, it is imperative that school complaints procedures should exist with a clear remit to address issues of bullying, so that children and parents can know they have a right to complain about inaction or inadequate action to safeguard children.

How to help

This book not only describes the research undertaken by ChildLine into bullying, it also outlines suggestions for tackling bullying - some from the children and adults we talked to on the lines and through the research; some from the experience ChildLine has built up from helping so many children and adults over the years; and some from good practice developed in schools and projects with which we have contact.

We have not hesitated to reiterate advice to be found elsewhere, because we want to disseminate as widely as possible the information which adults and children need in order to reduce and diminish the misery and fear which bullying engenders.

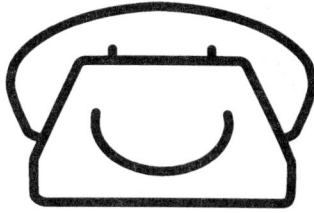

Chapter 2

Researching the line

Analysis of records from the Bullying Line

The Bullying Line was open from March to October 1994. It was mainly publicised through an intense social action campaign led by the BBC, involving local and national media including radio, TV and children's magazines, leading to extensive coverage throughout the media and with some direct publicity to schools (using posters). The response from children was phenomenal. The Line received a total of 58,530 calls; and from these 4,494 children and 691 adults were counselled, and there were over 770 follow-up counselling calls.

The discrepancy between the total calls figure and children counselled is usual for ChildLine. Like other helplines, ChildLine receives a large number of calls where children may initially have difficulty in beginning to talk. They may remain silent, speak only very briefly or use various means of testing the service before feeling confident enough to talk about what is worrying them. Some call several times before they are able to do so. When the lines are busy and there are no counsellors free to speak to the caller, he or she will be asked to call back. This explains why ChildLine **answers** significantly more children than it **counsels**. On average, there is a ratio of ten calls for every child counselled.

The conversations were all written up on a specifically designed case record, identifying a number of information areas for completion by counsellors. Recorded material was then put onto a database, factual/ quantitative information often being recorded in the form of codes at this point. Some of the areas identified for the database before the Bullying Line became operational included:

- the kind of bullying behaviour complained of
- main person(s) responsible for the bullying
- duration of the bullying
- location of the bullying
- child's emotional state
- action taken by the caller and others on his/her behalf.

Counsellors record the child's account of what has been happening to them, their feelings and actions in a narrative, using the child's own words as much as possible. This offers the researcher a rich source of direct testimony.

For the purposes of the research, a random sample of 1500 records was examined, almost half of those counselled between May and September 1994. Records were reviewed to ensure that all the existing information on the database was accurately recorded; to identify and record any further factual information which may have been missed in the initial coding exercise, and identify themes in the data or issues presented by children in the course of counselling.

Children calling

"I spend a lot of time crying in my room."

Calls to the Line came from all parts of the UK. Most children were reluctant to give details of their exact location or the schools they attended, and ChildLine Scotland had a separate bullying line funded by Tayside Regional Council running at the same time which reduced Scottish calls to the UK Bullying Line. So we cannot make any comment on regional variations in patterns of bullying. What we can say is that wherever children come from their words are strikingly the same.

Ages and gender of child callers

Children were usually willing to give their ages, though there was no data in seven per cent of the sample. Eighteen per cent of callers were aged ten and under; 56 per cent were between 11 and 13, and 18 per cent were 14 to 16. There were only three calls each from 17 and 18-year-olds. The following table gives a breakdown of the ages of boys and girls in the sample.

Table 1 – Bullying Line
Ages of children calling the line

Ages	Girls	%	Boys	%	Total	%
Unknown	91	*8*	12	*4*	103	*7*
5	1	*0*	0	*0*	1	*0*
6	3	*0*	3	*1*	6	*0*
7	11	*1*	5	*2*	16	*1*
8	17	*1*	7	*2*	24	*2*
9	55	*5*	28	*10*	83	*6*
10	101	*8*	27	*9*	128	*9*
11	184	*15*	43	*15*	227	*15*
12	262	*22*	49	*17*	311	*21*
13	249	*21*	50	*17*	299	*20*
14	137	*11*	35	*12*	172	*11*
15	65	*5*	17	*6*	82	*5*
16	32	*3*	10	*3*	42	*3*
17	1	*0*	2	*1*	3	*0*
18	3	*0*	0	*0*	3	*0*
Total	**1212**	*100*	**288**	*100*	**1500**	*100*

As the table shows, four times more girls than boys used the Line. The largest group of users were girls aged 11 to 14, making 55 per cent of all counselling calls.

This ratio of female to male callers is similar to that of ChildLine's main service. We do not think this relates to the incidence of bullying but to girls' and boys' willingness to use a helpline to talk about problems they have, suggesting that new strategies are required to encourage boys to ask for help. However, since incidence figures relate to how bullying is defined, this may also suggest that girls are more affected by forms of bullying which are excluded from 'adult' definitions, and that they only present their experience as bullying when they are free to name it themselves.

As the chart below shows, although boys overall used the Line in much smaller numbers than girls, younger boys (aged ten and under) were more likely to call than their female peers. Forty one per cent of male callers giving their age were of primary school age, compared with 33 per cent of female callers. Are younger boys bullied more or are they more able to say so? Our study suggests that as boys get older they learn how they are expected to behave as men and, as studies of adult males have shown, find it much harder than young women to ask for help.

Table 2 – Bullying Line
Age and gender breakdown of children calling the line

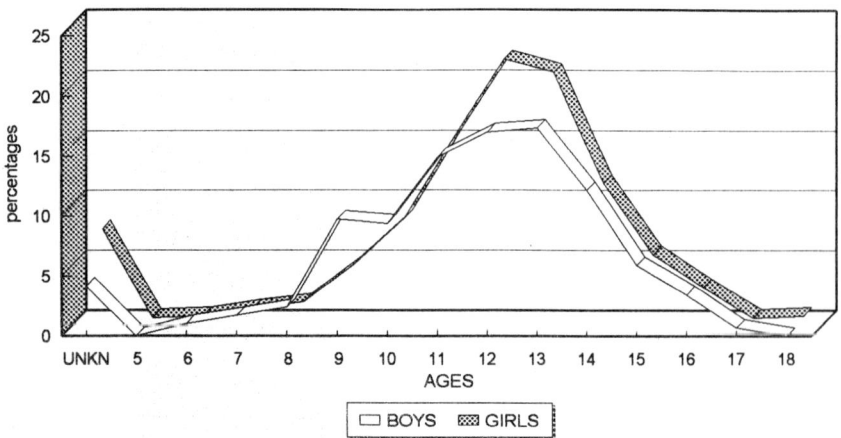

Family and living circumstances

Data on the family and living circumstances of children is very patchy. Only one in four children told us about their living circumstances; of these, nearly 90 per cent lived at home and just over ten per cent in foster or residential care or boarding school. Approximately 2.1 per cent of school age children are in boarding school or living in residential or foster care. The proportion of children ringing the Bullying Line living away from home indicates that they may be more likely to experience bullying or more isolated in dealing with it. The ChildLine study on children's experience of residential and foster care, Time to listen (1994) showed that bullying was the most common problem complained of by children in residential care, and that 35 per cent of runaways from care were running from bullying or violence. Bullying was also the most common problem identified by children (19%) ringing ChildLine's 1991 Boarding School Line.

Less than half of the child callers told us about their family circumstances; of those who did, 70 per cent were in two-parent and 28 per cent in one-parent families.

Ethnicity and disability

Children ringing ChildLine do not necessarily identify their race, cultural origin or disability. This is not something we ask of them, since they need the freedom to make their own declarations about their identity. Nor do we encourage counsellors to guess at children's ethnic origin or other aspects of children's lives. So we do not know what proportion of our callers are white, black, of mixed parentage, or from a minority ethnic group. Neither can we be certain how many callers suffer a disability.

Only two per cent of children in the call sample said that they were from a minority ethnic group. One per cent said they had a physical or mental disability of some kind. Nearly all these callers indicated that their bullying problem was directly related to their ethnic origin or disability.

Bystanders and 'Bullies'

The vast majority of children called because they were the victims of bullying. Only ten children from the sample of 1500 called about bullying others. A small but significant proportion of children in the sample (6%) called about a friend or relative who was being bullied. The majority of those callers (54%) who specified the kind of bullying their friends were suffering talked about physical attacks or threats of attack, followed by name-calling (21%) and teasing (16%).

Adults calling the Bullying Line

Over the six month period studied, 591 calls from adults were recorded. Of these, 270 were randomly selected for the research and reviewed in detail.

The overwhelming majority (87%) of adult calls came from women; often a child's mother or close female relative. While this may suggest that women tend to assume or be given the responsibility for dealing with their child's problems, it may be that women are more likely than men to ring for help in doing so.

Ninety-nine per cent of the sample (268) were about children being bullied, and most (40%) of these were about physical bullying. A further 14 per cent called about name-calling and nine per cent about incidents of teasing.

Table 3 – Bullying Line
Ages of the children adults were concerned about

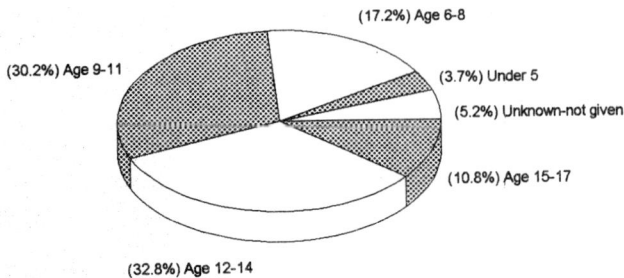

(17.2%) Age 6-8
(30.2%) Age 9-11
(3.7%) Under 5
(5.2%) Unknown-not given
(10.8%) Age 15-17
(32.8%) Age 12-14

Just over half (51%) of the calls from adults were about children under 12 years of age. Table 3 opposite shows the ages of the children about whom adults called the Line.

Twenty-one per cent of the children (39) whom adults rang about were younger than eight; of these, ten children were aged five or under.

Very young children bully and are bullied despite the level of supervision in playgroups, nurseries and infant classes. These are children who usually cannot independently phone a helpline and so ChildLine does not hear from this age group in great numbers. Nor is this an age group that the anti-bullying literature has addressed significantly. Yet, if 'taking it out on others' is a major cause of bullying behaviour (as children tell us), then younger children with less developed social skills and means of communicating and managing feelings are bound to be involved in nasty and mean behaviour towards each other. Prevention of bullying has to start here.

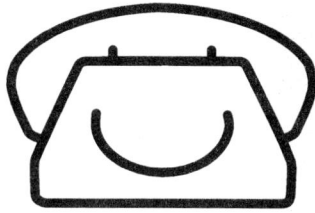

Chapter 3

Case study in schools

"I'd just like to say I think this questionnaire is very good. While I was writing this it made me think a lot about bullying. I don't know what this questionnaire is leading to but I hope the information you get helps you try and stop bullying."

This comment by a 14-year-old respondent to our questionnaire is encouraging. It shows that merely asking questions about bullying can open children's thinking and, therefore, the possibility of changing their environment. They can readily be engaged in this process and are potentially the most effective, if under-used, resource. Sadly, some schools, as we found, are still unwilling to ask the questions.

The case study in four schools was undertaken to provide a broader base of information and a comparison of children's perceptions with those of their teachers and, where possible, their parents, on the following issues:

- the level and frequency of bullying;
- the nature and effect of anti-bullying policies, and strategies for dealing with bullying;
- the most appropriate form of help for children who have been bullied.

It had been hoped that schools with and without a current anti-bullying policy, as well as those with a wide social mix, could be found to enable some exploration of the impact or otherwise of anti-bullying policies. This aim had to be abandoned, because all three schools we approached who were without a current policy refused to participate in the project. There was a shared fear that an exercise of this sort might stimulate acts of bullying and 'stir up' a problem which, it was believed, did not exist. Their responses illustrated the resistance to the subject of bullying persisting in some schools.

The four participating schools all had anti-bullying work underway. Two were primary schools – one with infants and juniors, the other a middle school catering for children aged eight to 11 years, both with around 300 pupils; and two were secondary schools, both large, with over 1,000 pupils aged between 11 and 18 years. All were co-educational.

Research work in the schools

The work in schools involved gathering information about each school's anti-bullying strategy and surveying attitudes to, and experiences of, bullying. Questionnaires were circulated to children (primary and secondary questionnaires were worded slightly differently to take account of age differences), their parents and staff in schools. Follow-up semi-structured interviews were conducted with a sample of the children who had been given the questionnaire.

The questionnaire and interviews addressed the following areas:
- definitions of bullying;
- experiences of being bullied, bystanding and bullying others;
- the level and frequency of bullying in the school;
- why bullying happens;
- location of bullying;
- how bullying can be reduced and stopped;
- how best to help children who had been bullied and those who bully.

The response rates to the questionnaire from each group were different: 63 per cent of children, 28 per cent of parents, and 13 per cent of teachers responded. Perhaps this, as much as anything, tells us the differing significance bullying has for children and adults.

The schools

The four schools which participated in the research project were based in London and the South East. They all had mixed catchment areas, including large housing estates and tree-lined avenues, bringing together in each school families from a variety of social backgrounds.

At that time, three of the schools had in operation a written anti-bullying policy or code of conduct, while the fourth had developed a comprehensive behaviour policy. All four schools were keen to tackle and reduce the level of bullying in their schools, demonstrated in their willingness to participate in a research project which might have brought them 'bad news' about their school.

All were extremely open and helpful in giving access to written materials about bullying and in discussing their approaches to tackling bullying. They assisted actively in arranging for the survey to be conducted, participating in the selection of students and the distribution and collection of questionnaires. The four participating schools were:

[2]**City Primary School:** Based in an inner city area with an ethnically diverse population, this school had some 300 pupils aged between 5 to 11, and 35 members of staff. City school had both a **statement on behaviour** and an **anti-bullying statement**. The behaviour statement was directed at staff in the school and outlined briefly how they could encourage appropriate behaviour in pupils. The anti-bullying statement was aimed at parents and their children. It encouraged parents to speak to their children about bullying and always to report bullying incidents to the school. It outlined the philosophy behind the school's behaviour policy. Parents and staff were guaranteed a sympathetic response to reports of bullying.

2 All names given to schools are fictitious to protect their identity.

Birchwood Secondary School: This was a large school located on the outskirts of a town. The catchment area was mixed and included a large housing estate. The school catered for 11 to 18-year-olds and had some 1300 pupils and over 100 staff. Birchwood had an anti-bullying policy aimed at pupils, and designated staff were assigned the responsibility for resolving reported bullying. The policy defined bullying as the school perceived it, outlined the expected code of behaviour in the school, encouraged children to report bullying, and promised that staff would act within a certain time limit to investigate and resolve complaints of bullying.

Sandwell Middle School: This was a small school based on the outskirts of a coastal town. The catchment area was socially mixed and largely white. The school catered for eight to 12- year-olds, had 320 pupils and 38 members of staff.

Sandwell had **an extensive behaviour policy which made specific reference to bullying**. The policy was aimed at all members of the school community, which it defined as children, parents and staff. It included a code of conduct for staff and another for children, and expectations of parental support. A system of rewards and sanctions was defined. The anti-bullying section spelt out the ways in which the school discouraged bullying and how bullying incidents would be dealt with. Advice for children who were being bullied was also included.

Lakeside Secondary School: This was another large school, based close to two towns, in a residential area. The school catered for 1200 pupils and had 119 staff. Lakeside served a socially mixed community and included people from ethnic minorities, mainly Asian.

The school had **a code of conduct** aimed at pupils, given to all children when they began school, but at that time no written anti-bullying policy as such. The subject was, however, raised regularly at assemblies, where pupils were informed that bullying would not be tolerated, and they were encouraged to tell staff about any incidents of bullying. The school had recently developed an extensive behaviour and anti-bullying policy which was to be introduced imminently.

Thus three of the schools, one primary (City), and two secondary (Birchwood and Lakeside) had in operation a fairly straightforward anti-bullying policy or code of conduct which focused on:

• encouraging children to tell about bullying;

• stating that staff would respond to a complaint of bullying (in one case within a specified time limit);

• outlining the main reasons why bullying was unacceptable behaviour.

These schools had devised some basic rules aimed at pupils, communicated by means of a poster and leaflet campaign in the school, through various articles, assemblies and meetings of parents.

Sandwell Middle school had adopted a distinctly different approach. The anti-bullying policy was enshrined in a comprehensive behaviour policy aimed at all members of the school community, including parents, staff and children. The behaviour policy specified:

• a code of conduct for adults and one for children;

• behaviour principles;

• a statement of what the anti-bullying policy meant in practice;

• advice for children who were being bullied;

• methods of: pastoral care, discipline (including rewards and sanctions) and 'first-aid' procedure;

• expectations of parents and their involvement in the school policy;

• a behaviour contract between the child, their parents and teacher.

This was the kind of policy Lakeside School was on the verge of implementing, negotiated through the various representative committees in the school, including the School Council which represented pupils.

The schools survey: respondents to the questionnaire

Children

Three hundred pupils in each school, representative of each school's population in terms of age, gender and ethnicity, were selected by school staff to be circulated with a questionnaire drawn up specifically for children. In the event one school (Lakeside) was unable to circulate 75 of the original 300 questionnaires.

Of the 1125 questionnaires circulated to children in the four schools, 714 children (63%) responded. The response rate from the secondary school children was higher than that from the primary schools: 494 secondary children compared with 220 primary school children, with slightly more boys responding in the secondary school and slightly more girls in the primary samples.

The ages and gender of the children are shown in table 4 opposite.

Boys and girls were more or less equally represented in the total sample and in each age group, which balances the picture emerging from the helpline.

Four per cent (30 children) did not say how old they were. Of those who did, 22 per cent were ten and under, compared with 18 per cent on the Line. There was a concentration of children in the 12 to 15 age group (with very few responses from 17 and 18- year-olds).

Most (82%) of the children described themselves as white, 14 per cent said they were from an ethnic minority group and described themselves variously as: Asian, black, West Indian, mixed race, Indian, Pakistani, Arab. Four per cent gave no information about their ethnic origin.

Staff responding

Three hundred and fifty-nine staff (including a number of ancillary and part-time workers) were circulated with a questionnaire asking about their perceptions of the level and extent of bullying in their

Table 4 – Surveyed Children

Age and gender breakdown of children who responded

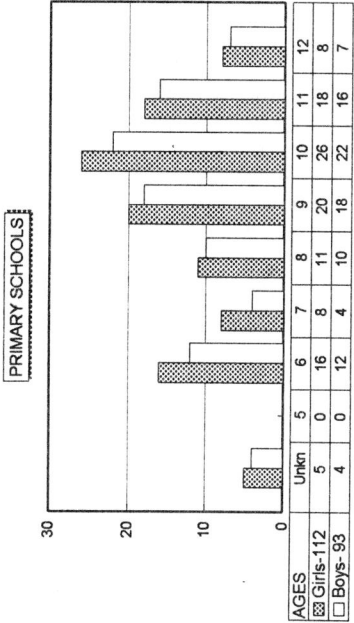

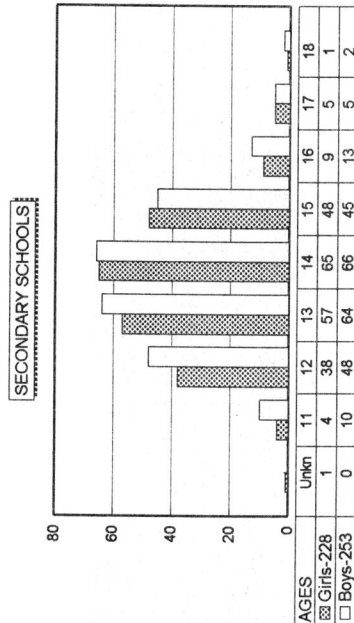

Primary schools (n=205)

Ages	Girls	%	Boys	%	Total	%
Unkn	5	4	4	4	9	4
5	0	0	0	0	0	0
6	16	14	12	13	28	14
7	8	7	4	4	12	6
8	11	10	10	11	21	10
9	20	18	18	19	38	19
10	26	23	22	24	48	23
11	18	17	16	17	34	17
12	8	7	7	8	15	7
Total	112	100	93	100	205	100

Secondary schools (n=481)

Ages	Girls	%	Boys	%	Total	%
Unkn	1	0	0	0	1	0
11	4	2	10	4	14	3
12	38	17	48	19	86	18
13	57	25	64	25	121	25
14	65	29	66	26	131	27
15	48	21	45	18	93	19
16	9	4	13	5	22	5
17	5	2	5	2	10	2
18	1	0	2	1	3	1
Total	228	100	253	100	481	100

school, how effective they thought the school approach was and how children could best be supported. Only 13 per cent (46) responded. The majority (91%) of those who did respond were teaching staff and 67 per cent (31) were female. They included staff with various specialist responsibilities in the school such as management or pastoral care.

Just over half of the respondents were from primary schools, and just under half from secondary. Since overall staff numbers were greater in the secondary schools, proportionately more staff from the primary schools responded.

Sixty one per cent (28 respondents) said they had personal experience of bullying. The majority, but not all, had been bullied at school; others considered themselves bullied in adult relationships at work or home.

Parents

The 1125 children circulated with a questionnaire were also given one for their parent(s)/main carers. In total, 320 parents/carers returned the questionnaire, a response rate of 28 per cent. Of these, 80 per cent were completed by women.

Most (89%) of the parents/carers said they were white; three per cent described themselves as from ethnic minority groups.

Compared with the staff respondents, fewer parents (37%) indicated they had personal experience of bullying. Of those who did, most had been bullied at school, but a few considered other adults had bullied them in their personal relationships or at work.

A third of the respondents (107) stated their child had been bullied in the last year, whereas 64 per cent of primary school and 45 per cent of secondary school respondents said they had been bullied.

Children interviewed

The intention was to interview about ten per cent of the children surveyed in each school (120 children). In the event a lower number

(107) were interviewed, using a brief interview schedule which covered the same areas as those in the questionnaire. The interviews were informal and conducted as a structured conversation with a child. Just under half of those interviewed were in primary school and just over half in secondary. The ages and gender of the children interviewed in each sector are summarised in the table below.

Table 5 – Children Interviewed
Age Breakdown

Primary schools

Ages	Girls	%	Boys	%	Total	%
Age 5/6 years	5	19	5	20	10	20
Age 7 years	4	15	1	4	5	10
Age 8 years	4	15	3	12	7	13
Age 9 years	6	22	8	32	14	27
Age 10 years	6	22	2	8	8	15
Age 11 years	2	7	6	24	8	15
TOTAL	27	100	25	100	52	100

Secondary schools

Ages	Girls	%	Boys	%	Total	%
Age 12 years	10	36	5	18	15	28
Age 13 years	3	11	6	21	9	16
Age 14 years	4	15	5	18	9	16
Age 15 years	5	19	5	18	10	18
Age 16 years	4	15	5	18	9	17
Age 17 years	1	4	2	7	3	5
TOTAL	27	100	28	100	55	100

Boys and girls were again equally represented among the children interviewed. As the chart shows, the age distribution of interviewees was slightly uneven. The majority (86%) of children described themselves as white; 14 per cent said they were from an ethnic minority group. Only two of the children interviewed said they had a disability.

A very high proportion (79%) of the children interviewed said they had been bullied at some point at the school they currently attended. Researchers exploring incidence levels on adult reports of child sexual abuse have also found that following up questionnaires with interviews produces a higher incidence rate as more experiences are remembered (Kelly et al, 1991, Russell, 1984). Boys and girls were again roughly equally represented among those children who had been bullied. Fifty-two per cent were in primary schools.

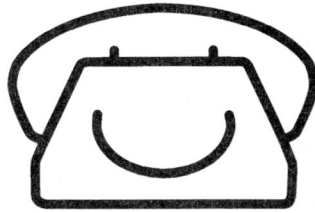

Chapter 4

What is bullying?

"It's pushing and calling names, saying they're going to hit you."

"Being nasty to people and making their lives a misery."

"Picking on a person, taking the mick out of them, taking advantage, like if they want something they're just going to get it, otherwise they'll hurt you or something."

"Punching, hitting, spreading rumours about people, name-calling, blackmail."

"People getting picked on – either name-calling or whatever. It's bullying if the person who's actually getting called names is getting disturbed by it."

The nature of bullying

These are a flavour of the children's responses to the interview question: what would you call bullying? Adult definitions are different. They feature in the anti-bullying policies and research studies. Many specifically refer to prolonged duration and frequent incidence as characteristic features of bullying. Roland (1988), for example, described bullying as longstanding violence against people who cannot defend themselves. Olweus (1991) defines bullying thus:

"A student is being bullied or victimised when he or she is exposed, repeatedly and over time, to negative actions on the part of one or more students."

Tattum (1993) writes of bullying as wilful and conscious and Smith (1994) as a systematic abuse of power. The DFE pack (1994) sums up the common features in adult definitions as:

"- it is deliberately hurtful behaviour,

- it is repeated often over a period of time,

- it is difficult for those being bullied to defend themselves."

Children describe a more complex picture. Their accounts to the 1990 Bullying Line (La Fontaine 1991) challenged the basis of many adult definitions of bullying. The 1994 Line confirms this.

Children and young people do not always describe bullying as **repeated** or longstanding. Many acknowledge it can be unintentional as well as intentional, that it can be indiscriminate and random as well as systematic, and that any child is vulnerable to becoming a target as well as those less able to defend themselves. The bullying that children describe experiencing, and participating in, is both more straightforward and more subtle than adult definitions allow. Children highlight the complex interplay of factors involved in the initiation and progression of acts of bullying and particularly demonstrate bullying as arbitrary, casual and frightening, as well as intentional and orchestrated.

Children calling the Line and those interviewed in schools did not see duration and frequency as central to definitions of bullying. They were more likely to emphasise what was actually done, their own response to it and their understanding of the bullies' motivations. While most child callers describe longstanding and repeated bullying, others indicate that just one act may be sufficient to trigger the feelings of powerlessness, fear and anxiety characteristic of the effects of bullying.

Individual children respond in different ways to similar acts of bullying and the same child may respond differently at different times and in different contexts. Their responses, in turn, have an impact on the course of subsequent events and on children's feelings about themselves and the incident or incidents.

Although children recognise that bullying may indeed involve an intention to hurt another child, particularly in cases of physical attack, they also perceive that, on occasions, bullies may be unaware of the effects of their actions. As Michelle, a 14-year-old, described during an interview:

> *"If say you're mucking around you can make comments but not really mean to hurt them, like if you're joking around and you think they'll find it funny, but they might not, they might take it to heart."*

The distinctive feature of children's descriptions is their perception of the spiralling nature of bullying behaviour. Children in this study consistently described the first act of bullying as holding the potential threat of a deteriorating pattern which may culminate in physical attack: what starts as teasing and verbal taunts may escalate into habitual bullying which may become physical. This perception presumably arises from their observation of bullying behaviour and accounts for the level of fear which one act can inspire. Philip (15) during interview described this process at work:

> *"It started off with name-calling and that sort of thing and in the end it got more difficult, a bit physical and that. You know if you're called names you sort of wait and see if it's the usual sort of thing that happens but it didn't, it got worse."*

The extent to which the bullying proceeds along this route seems to be influenced by a number of factors, including the motivations of the bully, the response of the bullied child and other children, the level of supervision and the rules of behaviour governing the environment in which the exchange occurs. But children appear to experience it as random and unpredictable which adds, of course, to their fear.

Types of bullying

Children surveyed

The children surveyed were asked to tick which behaviour they thought was bullying from the list outlined in table 6, opposite. Though all the possibilities were ticked by some respondents, not all categories were ticked by all. They were most likely to tick extortion, hitting, name-calling and threatening, and less likely to tick teasing and spreading rumours, with 'excluding' receiving least. Girls were more likely than boys to tick 'excluding' and spreading rumours.

Those children surveyed who said they were bullied in the past year were asked what kind of bullying they had experienced. All those categories ticked by children in table 6 featured. Forty three per cent of the bullied children in primary school and 53 per cent in secondary had experienced more than one kind of bullying, and 33 per cent of children had experienced physical bullying: hitting, punching or kicking.

Out of the whole primary sample (220), 18 per cent (41 children) had been hit, punched or kicked, but only five per cent (27 children) of the secondary sample (494). In both groups boys received more physical bullying than girls. Table 7, overleaf shows the bullying pattern in each sector, supporting the evidence from other studies that the incidence of physical bullying declines and name-calling increases as children get older. Interestingly though, incidence of the less serious forms of physical bullying - throwing, pushing and pulling - is similar, and the level of threats of violence increases with age.

Table 6 – Surveyed Children
How surveyed children defined bullying

Primary schools

	Girls	%	Boys	%	Total	%
Name calling	93	83	72	77	165	80
Spreading rumours	79	71	49	53	128	62
Extortion	102	91	81	87	183	89
Threats	95	85	80	86	175	85
Teasing	80	71	66	71	146	71
Hitting	102	91	87	94	189	92
Pushing/pulling/throwing	97	87	80	86	177	86
Excluding	63	56	36	39	99	48
Total completed Q/T's	112		93		205	

Secondary schools

	Girls	%	Boys	%	Total	%
Name calling	212	93	221	87	433	90
Spreading rumours	123	54	111	44	234	49
Extortion	215	94	237	94	452	94
Threats	193	85	213	84	406	84
Teasing	176	77	165	65	341	71
Hitting	220	96	244	96	464	96
Pushing/pulling/throwing	205	90	213	84	418	87
Excluding	77	34	58	23	135	28
Total completed Q/T's	228		253		481	

Table 7 – Surveyed Children
How surveyed children were bullied

Primary schools

	Girls	%	Boys	%	Total	%
Name calling	14	30	13	31	27	30
Rumours	3	6	0	0	3	3
Extortion	2	4	2	5	4	4
Threats	1	2	1	2	2	2
Teasing	4	9	5	12	9	10
Hitting/physical attack	18	38	23	55	41	46
Pushing/pulling/throwing	13	28	9	21	22	25
Excluding	8	17	2	5	10	11
Total responses	47		42		89	

Secondary schools

	Girls	%	Boys	%	Total	%
Name calling	39	62	20	41	59	53
Rumours	10	16	3	6	13	12
Extortion	5	8	8	16	13	12
Threats	12	19	6	12	18	16
Teasing	8	13	4	8	12	11
Hitting/physical attack	11	17	16	33	27	24
Pushing/pulling/throwing	14	22	13	27	27	24
Excluding	2	3	0	0	2	2
Total responses	63		49		112	

Children calling the Line

The picture presented by children calling the Line is similar, though, as one might expect, the proportion of children complaining about physical bullying was higher than in the school survey. Many children had experienced more than one kind of bullying, with 49 per cent of callers (46% of girls and 62% of boys), 687 children in all, describing physical attacks. Had the proportions of boys and girls calling the line been equal, extrapolating from the incidence of physical bullying among boys, the rate would of course be higher at around 54 per cent.

Table 8 – Bullying Line
How children calling the line were bullied

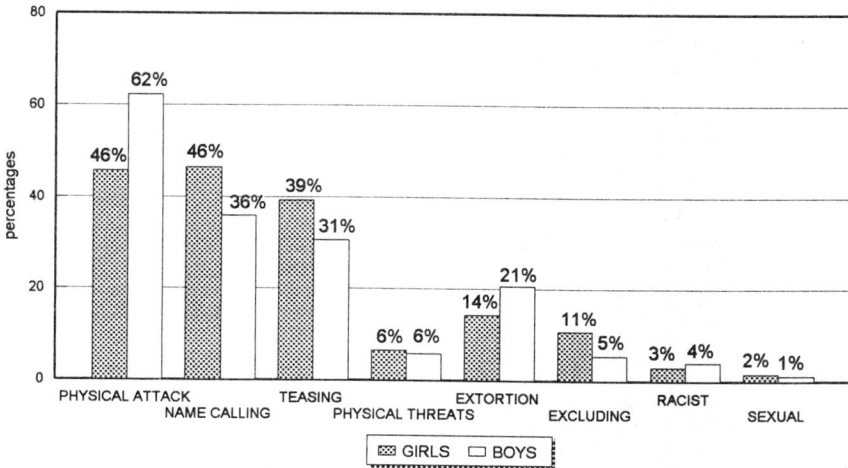

Main type of bullying

Although children calling the lines often complained about a number of different forms of bullying from the same bully(ies), they usually identified one particular type as the main problem about which they had called, and it is this breakdown of types of bullying which forms the basis of the analysis in the following table. It shows the breakdown in detail, with separate tables for boys and girls because bullying behaviour among boys and girls is different. Twenty-seven per cent of children counselled said that being hit, kicked or physically attacked was their **main** bullying problem. There was a gender difference here: 22 per cent of girls compared with 43 per cent of boys complained of physical attacks; and more primary school age boys reported physical attacks (53%). The rate of physical bullying found from callers is skewed by the fact that girls were so heavily represented among the callers (four girls to each boy caller). Had the ratios been similar the rate would most probably have been around 33 per cent of children.

Table 9 – Bullying Line
Main bullying problems given by children calling the line

	Girls	%	Boys	%	Total	%
Hitting/physical attack	258	23	121	43	379	27
Name Calling	290	26	50	18	340	24
Teasing	108	10	42	15	150	11
Threats/physical attack	108	10	10	4	118	8
Pushing/pulling/throwing	90	8	16	6	106	8
Extortion	58	5	15	5	73	5
Non-specific bullying	46	4	9	3	55	4
Excluding behaviour	50	4	2	1	52	4
Spreading rumours	41	4	1	0	42	3
Stealing possessions	24	2	7	2	31	2
Racist bullying	23	2	5	2	28	2
Other verbal abuse	11	1	0	0	11	1
A bully	8	1	2	1	10	1
Risk of being bullied	6	1	1	0	7	0
Bystander	1	0	0	0	1	0
Total	1122	100	281	100	1403	100

A further eight per cent of girls and six per cent of boys complained mainly of being thrown, pushed or pulled around, and ten per cent of girls and four per cent of boys of being threatened with physical attack. In all, then, physical bullying and threatening behaviour accounted for 40 per cent of girls' complaints and 53 per cent of boys'.

Name-calling was the main concern of 25 per cent of girls and 18 per cent of boys (24% of the whole sample) while the third most common problem was teasing (11% of all children) complained of by ten per cent of the girls and 15 per cent of the boys. Together these three forms of bullying accounted for 80 per cent of the problems presented by children calling the Line.

Name-calling

> *"If it's physical, it'll be like a cut then go away; if you're being called names it stays with you, you can't really put it out of your mind," said one ten year-old boy.*

> *"I was made a fool of in the class today, called a spastic and a mongol and the teacher laughed. I felt so humiliated. I am very angry with the teachers for letting these boys get away with it," said James, aged 15.*

Children commonly describe the first act of bullying as name-calling or 'teasing'. Name-calling as distinct from other forms of 'teasing' is characterised by the bully or bullies focusing on one aspect of the individual's physique, personality or behaviour or using terms of abuse which can be racist, sexual or to do with disability, and which may or may not apply to the child. On the Bullying Line children most often described being called names reflecting a physical attribute – being fat or thin, tall or short, having red hair, big ears, protruding teeth, acne and so on. Name-calling relating to their ethnicity, colour, disablement, or background was also mentioned.

Any distinctive feature of a child could be the focus for name-calling. Bullies might identify a real or perceived aspect of the child's personality, so that a child who, for instance, worked hard or was seen to have a lot of relationships with the opposite sex, or simply behaved slightly outside the 'acceptable' norms, might be the subject of name-calling.

Children sometimes felt that one particular incident had provoked it, as in the case of Kathy, a 14-year-old girl who told a counsellor:

> *"I accidentally got my hand caught in another girl's swimming costume when we were changing for swimming, and since then she's been calling me lesbian and that."*

Others believed there was some real basis for the names they were called. Children who were overweight or spotty often acknowledged the fact, but remained confused about why the bully/bullies had started to pick on **them,** particularly when others with the same characteristics were not being singled out.

Most children being bullied in this way agonised over why it was happening to them. Children who had been bullied over a long period often felt hopeless about their ability to stop the bullying; many felt in some way responsible for the fact that they were being bullied. However confident children felt about themselves, being subjected to long periods of name-calling left them feeling that there was something 'wrong' with them. **The damage to their self-confidence and self-esteem required considerable attention as well as action to put an end to the abuse.**

'Teasing' [3]

> *"The things they say to me feel like a dagger in my back,"*
> *said ten-year-old Mark.*

Eleven per cent of the children calling the Line complained that they were being 'teased'. Interestingly, this was more commonly complained of by boys than girls. Girls also described being left out and other children whispering or spreading rumours about them (a further eight per cent), while hardly any boys did (just one per cent). Children used the term teasing to describe more general acts of verbal bullying. Although name-calling was one feature of these calls, teasing generally encompassed more sustained jibes and taunts. A typical example was that of Joe, who had a large mole on his cheek:

> *Joe called the Bullying Line because the bullies were teasing him about the mole, saying it was a love bite from his Mum. Joe had tried to ignore them, but the bullies kept following him around and it was really beginning to get him down.*

Although name-calling and teasing overlap, teasing seems to be an extension of simple name-calling into a more elaborate and sustained attack on the child, exploiting the implications or

---

3 The word 'teasing' does not necessarily reflect the seriousness of the pestering behaviour children experience. Harassment would perhaps be a more accurate term. However, since children themselves use this word to describe this form of bullying, it has been retained in the text.

consequences of a physical attribute, characteristic or feature of the child's life which is the focus of the harassment. The cruelty involved can be severe. One child whose father had killed himself reported being teased about that.

Other children were being teased about their family circumstances or specific aspects of their lives - being adopted or in local authority care, living with a single parent, not 'going out' in the evenings, not having a boy or girl friend or being sexually unaware. Many of the issues children were teased about did not necessarily lend themselves to one simple category of bullying. Some of the teasing appeared to function as peer pressure to force conformity to peer group norms of behaviour: smoking, drinking, sexual activity or even, in a few cases, drug use.

Physically threatening behaviour

> *"A gang of girls are bullying me at school. They pick on me, pull my hair and push me around. They tell the teacher I've been doing naughty things. My mum told the teacher and the girls were told off; but they've started again. My dad says I have to fight my own battles."* Kerry is ten years old.

Sixteen per cent of children rang because their main problem was being pushed around or intimidated by threats of violence. Children talked of being pushed, pulled, shoved, thrown around, squashed, followed, chased and having clothes, bags or hair pulled. They were threatened with being 'got', beaten up at some later time. This form of bullying was usually described by children as part of a campaign of harassment which might also involve name-calling, teasing, or having things taken away.

Pushing, pulling, and jostling can be hard to distinguish from play fighting, and often take place while children are under adult supervision. Adults seem to see it as normal rough and tumble and indeed, the children involved in doing it may be unaware of just how nasty it feels. Many children described similar responses to that of Kerry's father. Hugh, 12 years old, told us his father thought he needed to stand up for himself more. Peter, aged nine, said his teacher told him to toughen up, that he was too sensitive. This kind of reaction from adults leaves children feeling abandoned to the bullies and less able to approach adults for help.

The depth of fear inspired in children was severe, as they awaited each day's events. Jack, who was 12, felt unable to face going to school. He had thought of breaking his arm or jumping out of the window to avoid it. Alice, aged 13, got stomach aches, was frightened to go to school. She said she felt like killing herself.

Physical attacks

> *"I am at the stage of wanting to die instead of going to school," said Alex. He is 11 and is hit and kicked repeatedly.*

Bullying was only categorised by ChildLine as physical attack when the bullied child had been beaten, hit, kicked or punched with or without a weapon.

While the same percentage of girls complained about physical attacks as in the 1990 study, there was an increase of 12 per cent (from 31% to 43%) in the percentage of boys who said they had been attacked. Given that the definition in the current study is more rigorous, this may be an underestimate for both boys and girls; however, it would be unwise to infer that there is a significant general increase in violent bullying without further research.

Children described a range of physical injuries, from bruising to broken limbs. They talked of being punched, kicked or hit with various objects but most commonly 'battered' or 'beaten up' by one or more, often several, children. As might be expected, physical attacks were more likely to occur in those areas where there was less adult supervision.

> *Sophie (11) called about being bullied by Julie, another girl in her class. It had started after some of the boys in their class had called Julie a slag. Sophie said, "She doesn't*

do it at school; she waits till we're on the school bus, then she hits me." Sophie had recently received a black eye from one of these attacks and had told her teacher. The teacher had advised her to try to sort it out herself.

Although most children had been attacked more than once, six per cent (23 children) had been so frightened that they had called the Line after the first attack.

Gender seems to play an important part: girls are less likely than boys to experience or proceed to physically attacking behaviour. (Nearly twice as many surveyed primary and secondary boys as girls complaining of bullying said they had been physically attacked.) Nevertheless this does not mean that girls do not **threaten** to bully others physically - indeed from the cases on the Bullying Line proportionately more girls (10%) than boys (3.5%) were reported to have threatened other children in the course of bullying.

Age is also significant. Information from the 1994 Bullying Line confirmed the 1991 finding that reports of physical bullying decrease as children get older; 56 per cent of children under seven and a third of the eight to ten year olds called about physical bullying. (See graph overleaf.) For children over 14 this figure dropped to a quarter. This finding might be interpreted as reluctance on the part of older children to report bullying and/or the low proportion of boys calling the Line. But the school survey confirmed this pattern.

Broken friendships and bullying

"What hurts me so much is that she used to be my friend."

A distinct kind of bullying described by child callers arose from broken friendships. Eighteen per cent of children counselled had previously been friends with the bully. Bullying of this kind was more likely to be reported by girls than boys, 21 per cent of girls calling compared with nine per cent of boys. Typically children had fallen out with a friend over something and the resulting animosity had developed into bullying initiated by one of them.

Table 10 – Bullying Line
Main bullying problem –
age and gender breakdown of children calling the line

Girls

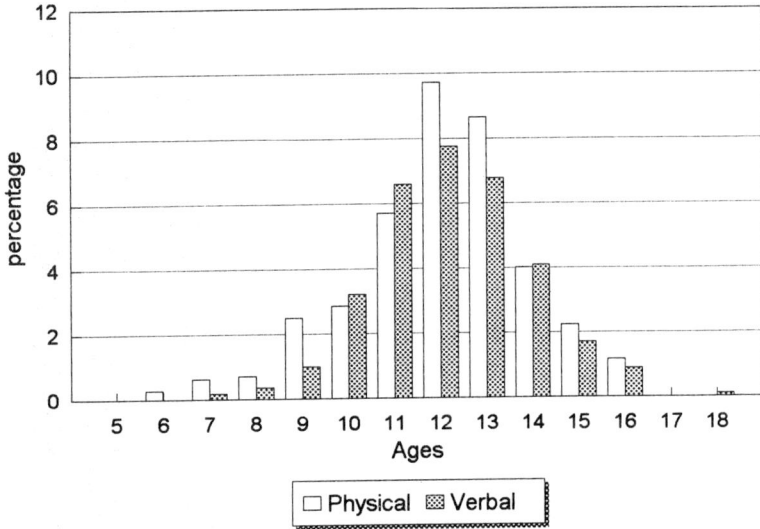

Boys

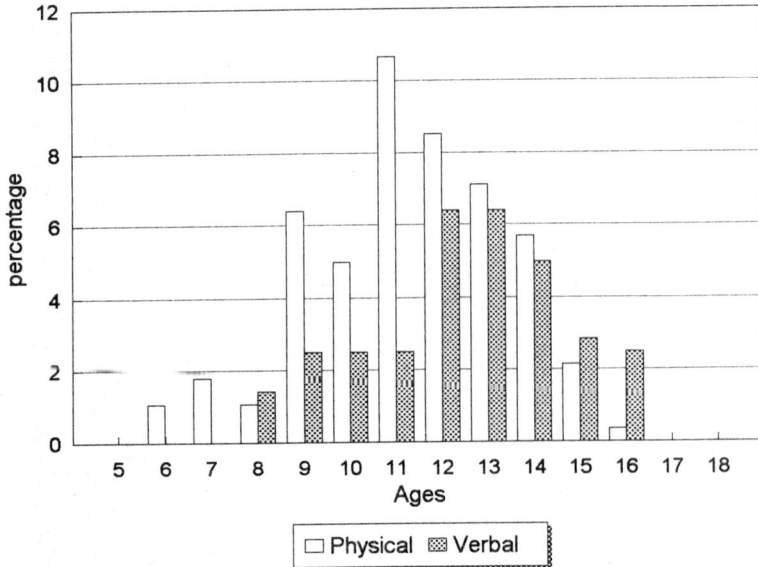

Children interviewed often discussed how arguments with friends could develop into bullying. Those surveyed most commonly ascribed the origins of bullying to disputes and arguments. Arguments might be about other relationships, falling out about boyfriends and girlfriends or issues such as who was sitting next to whom.

Children under eight described this process of making and breaking friends as being very common, often based on what they were going to play in the playground, who was 'in charge' of the game and who could play or not.

This type of bullying illustrates well that anti-bullying strategies must focus on improving children's social skills, particularly their ability to negotiate disagreements. Traditionally, free unstructured play among children is viewed positively as offering children the opportunity to learn from experience about how to 'become social'. It is clear to us from children's experiences of bullying that they cannot be entirely left to find out by experience, because there are inevitably casualties: those who end up being left out. Adults need to organise at times, and to supervise, from a distance, and through their observation of changing relationships among children, help them to manage their social relations without bullying each other.

Racist bullying

"I am the only Asian in the class. They have started calling me 'Paki' all the time ... I don't know why, maybe it's because I do well in exams ... I don't want to tell my mum and dad. It would upset them too much."

Although the number of children known to be from minority ethnic groups calling the Bullying Line was relatively small (30 in the sample) 93 per cent cited a racist related bullying problem. Some of the bullying they had experienced was very disturbing.

Claudette is 14. She is bullied because her dad is black and her mum is white. She is called names but recently a group of children attacked her outside school and broke her nose.

The police were involved and gave them a warning. She is terrified it will happen again.

Dean is 13. He is bullied by a group of white boys in and out of school. He is called names and hit and kicked. A crowd of them collected outside his house recently and his mum called the police. Now they say they will get him for that. He is very afraid.

Children described feeling very isolated, particularly where they attended a school where there were few similar children. The impact the bullying can have on children's self-esteem was shown by Jackie (13) who told the counsellor that she felt like killing herself and wished she were white.

The problem of racist bullying may well be much more widespread than the experience of the Bullying Line suggests. Nearly a third (31%) of the children responding to the survey in schools identified black children and other minority groups as those who are more likely to be picked on by bullies. For example, Harry, a white eight-year-old, who explained, when asked at interview why he thought bullies picked on people:

"Cause they don't like them, their skin colour, they come from another country and speak a different language."

The response to the survey did not reveal that children from minority groups had experienced more bullying in the past than white children. In fact, 50 per cent of both groups reported having been bullied at some point, and 32 per cent of each group reported being bullied that year. But the sample of black and ethnic minority children was very small compared with the sample of white children and the figures must be viewed with caution.

Bullying disabled children

"They call me like something to do with my hearing aid, like deaf bastard or something, but I just go 'Oh, shut up'.

I feel like I can look after myself now but before at primary school, when I was smaller, I felt a bit hurt and I told a teacher and they tried moving us away from the other kids but that didn't work,"

said Colin (16) who had experienced this kind of bullying throughout his school years. The two disabled children interviewed had both experienced bullying which focused specifically on their disability. Seventeen children calling the Line said they were being bullied because they were disabled. Of course, telephone helplines cannot be used by many disabled children; the figure reflects this. Children with communication difficulties require special attentiveness from the adults around them to ensure that any bullying they experience is noticed and can be dealt with.

Children's concern for others

"The school is not interested ... I don't know what to do."

Ninety-seven children in the call sample rang with a concern about a friend or relative. Eighty-two of these callers were the friend of a child being bullied. Most (57%) were aged between 12 and 14, and 93 per cent of the calls were made by girls.

Children calling about others talked about all types of bullying, but a third were worried about another child's safety because of physical attack. Like many of the adult callers, these children wanted to do something to help, but did not know how to go about it. Many felt the school either could not or would not solve the problem. A typical example was Fran (14) calling about her friend Donna:

Donna was being continually harassed by two boys at school. They were calling her names and kept grabbing her breasts. Recently, they started to thump her. Donna's parents had told her to thump them back. Fran said the school was not interested in hearing about it. Donna had been telling Fran all about her problems, but Fran told the counsellor, 'I don't know what to do'.

49

Calls from adults

> *Sheila called the Bullying Line about her daughter, who was being subjected to what she described as 'daily verbal torture' by two girls who used to be friendly with her. She had reported the matter to the headteacher who had put Julie in front of the school during assembly and asked the bullies to stand up. Since then the bullying had intensified. Julie was becoming hysterical about going to school and had refused to allow her parents to talk to the school. Her mother was desperately worried about her and said Julie was becoming rude and uncommunicative.*

The majority (93%) of adult callers were parents calling because their own children were being bullied. Nearly all (71%) of these were concerned about the fact that their child's school had been unable to resolve the problem. Some schools had refused to acknowledge that there was a problem or had insisted that the bullied child had 'over-reacted' in some way. More commonly, the child was experiencing a persistent problem of bullying which his or her school had failed to stop, despite attempts to do so - either the bullying had stopped, but only temporarily, or it had just continued as before. In a few cases (6) it had actually got worse. Other parents called the Line about the effects bullying was having on their child; most were seeking advice on how to support their children and what action they could take on their behalf. Parents and other adults described how anxious, angry or despairing they felt. In 31 cases (10% of the adult sample) the parents seemed to have exhausted all the avenues available to them in the school. A few (18) had become so exasperated with the schools concerned that they had felt forced to withdraw their children.

Many parents were apprehensive about approaching the school, either because they were not sure how the staff would react or were anxious that the bullying might intensify if they complained. Others were anxious about an approach because they had complained about bullying before.

The schools these adults described appeared to be ineffective at dealing with problems of bullying. Some of these were reported to be reluctant to receive any reports of bullying, preferring to perceive it as 'normal', or an inevitable part of school life which just had to be accepted. Parents were particularly distressed when schools had reacted to a report of bullying by telling them their child was over-sensitive or that they themselves were being over-protective.

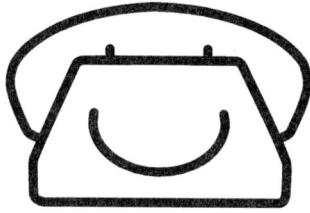

Chapter 5

When, where and how often does it happen?

How common was bullying in the schools?

According to our survey of children, bullying in schools is commonplace, even in schools with anti-bullying policies in place: 64 per cent of primary school children and 45 per cent of secondary children (38% of boys and 52% of girls) said they had been bullied at **some point** in their schools. Half (50%) of the primary school children and more than one in four (27%) of the secondary children responding said they had been bullied in **the last year**.

As expected, boys and girls were equally represented in the primary group; but proportionately more girls (31%) than boys (22%) in secondary school said they had been bullied in the past year. This is a very high level of reported bullying, but in keeping with findings from a recent action research project in schools, Pitts and Smith (1996).

Whitney and Smith (1993) in the Sheffield study found that one in four primary pupils and one in ten secondary pupils reported being bullied sometimes. But their study offered children a definition of bullying and excluded those who said it had only happened once or twice. If ChildLine withdrew from its figures those who had been bullied for a few days, then the numbers would come close to those of Whitney and Smith: 25 per cent primary and 13 per cent secondary. But this would not tell children's experience of bullying, and would elide from recognition the one-off and short bursts of bullying which children say cause them great fear. ChildLine asked children to say what they considered bullying to be before asking whether they had been bullied or had bullied others.

ChildLine's survey also had a higher figure for children admitting to bullying others: 18 per cent of primary and 25 per cent of secondary pupils reported bullying others that school year, compared with 12 per cent and six per cent respectively in the Sheffield study. Incidence studies of bullying, like those of sexual abuse (Kelly et al, 1991), will produce figures which vary according to definition; trying to find the 'true' level of bullying is, in the end, a fool's errand. What our survey shows is how **children** rate their experience of bullying and being bullied. It bears out the experience of other studies which indicate that where openness about bullying exists over time, then children are not only more able to report bullying but, it seems, more able to admit to it.

It also seems that adults' estimates of the frequency of bullying behaviour differ from that of children. In response to the question 'How often do you think bullying happens in your school?', children, parents and staff were asked to say whether they thought it happened: very often, often, sometimes or hardly ever. Children were twice as likely as adults to say bullying happened very often.

Duration of bullying

Of those children calling the Line who did give information about the duration of their problem (1066), most (48%) had been bullied for over a month and up to a year (see following table). A quarter of callers had been bullied for over one year; and three per cent (34 children) describing bullying which had persisted for more than five years. Twenty seven per cent had been bullied for less than a month.

Children surveyed presented a much less dismal picture as shown in table 12, overleaf. The majority (50% of primary and 45% secondary children) had been bullied for a few days and nearly 21 per cent a few weeks, showing that children calling the Bullying Line were in greater difficulty and less likely to be able to get

Table 11 – Bullying Line
Duration of bullying from call sample (excluding third party calls)

	Girls	%	Boys	%	Total	%
Unspecified	275		62		337	
Less than one week	52	6	13	5	65	6
Over a week, less then a month	189	22	32	15	221	21
Over a month, less than a year	427	50	87	40	514	48
One year - five years	156	19	76	35	232	22
Over five years	23	3	11	5	34	3
TOTAL	847	100	219	100	1066	100

effective help within their schools, and suggesting that children being bullied in schools with anti-bullying policies suffer for shorter periods of time.

Frequency of bullying

Many children surveyed who said they were bullied 'this year' described frequent bullying even if the bullying did not go on for long. Forty six per cent of primary and 43 per cent of secondary school children described being bullied several times a week. However, 37 per cent of primary and 43 per cent of secondary children said the bullying occurred occasionally or not very often.

Where bullying happens

Over three quarters of the bullying reported to the Line was taking place in and around the school. However 15 per cent of children reported being bullied in the local neighbourhood, compared with nine per cent in 1990. This group did not include children who were being bullied on the way to or from school (seven per cent of children). This finding may of course be influenced by the fact that the Bullying Line was operating over the summer holiday period as

Table 12 – Surveyed Children
Duration of bullying

Primary schools

	Girls	%	Boys	%	Total	%
Unspecified	61		50		111	
Days	29	56	19	44	48	51
Weeks	10	20	10	23	20	21
Months	6	12	6	14	12	13
All term	0	0	3	7	3	3
All year	6	12	5	12	11	12
Total	51	100	43	100	94	100

Secondary schools

	Girls	%	Boys	%	Total	%
Unspecified	156		194		350	
Days	31	43	28	47	59	45
Weeks	15	21	13	22	28	21
Months	14	19	8	14	22	17
All term	12	17	8	14	20	15
All year	0	0	2	3	2	2
Total	72	100	59	100	131	100

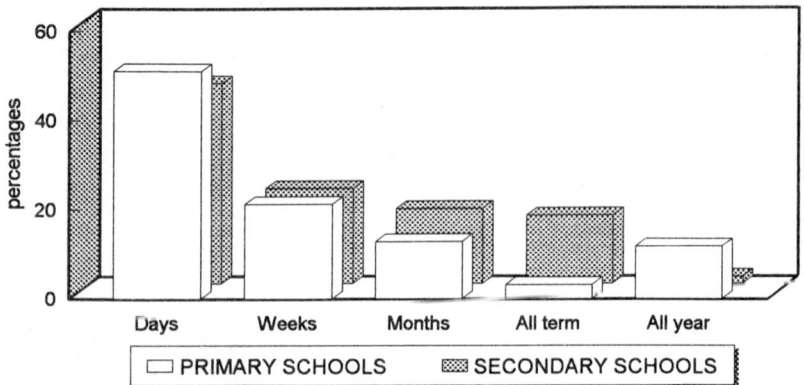

well as in term time. However, 17 per cent of the children taking part in the schools' survey also identified the local neighbourhood as a place where they encountered bullying. If more bullying is now actually taking place out of the school, it may be that the greater effectiveness of monitoring and challenging bullying behaviour in the schools has simply driven the problem outside the school gates! As one pessimistic respondent to the survey said:

"You can't stop bullying in school, because you'd just get bullied after school or in town or something."

Another indicated that supervision deterred physical bullying in school, saying:

"A lot of like name-calling and that sort of thing is done inside school and most physical things happen outside. But a lot of that's a result of what happens inside, which obviously you'd be pretty stupid to, like, beat someone up on the school premises."

Cases of bullying in the local area typically involved a child being picked on at the weekend, in a local youth club or a local park. These children had found it particularly difficult to get help in resolving their bullying problem, seemingly because many schools were reluctant to intervene in cases of bullying which had not taken place in or around the school grounds, even when pupils from their school were the 'culprits'. Children and parents are hesitant about involving the police and, when they try, they may not get help; and they also feel fearful of contacting the children concerned or their parents.

On the Line children identified a number of specific sites within the precincts of school where bullying took place. Most commonly these were the playground/recreation area and in the classroom. This finding was similar to that in ChildLine's schools survey where 65 per cent in all - 85 per cent primary and 46 per cent of secondary students - cited the playground. Children also identified the classroom and corridors as areas of frequent bullying, as outlined in table 13 overleaf (note that children are bullied in more than one

Table 13 – Surveyed Children
Where children were bullied

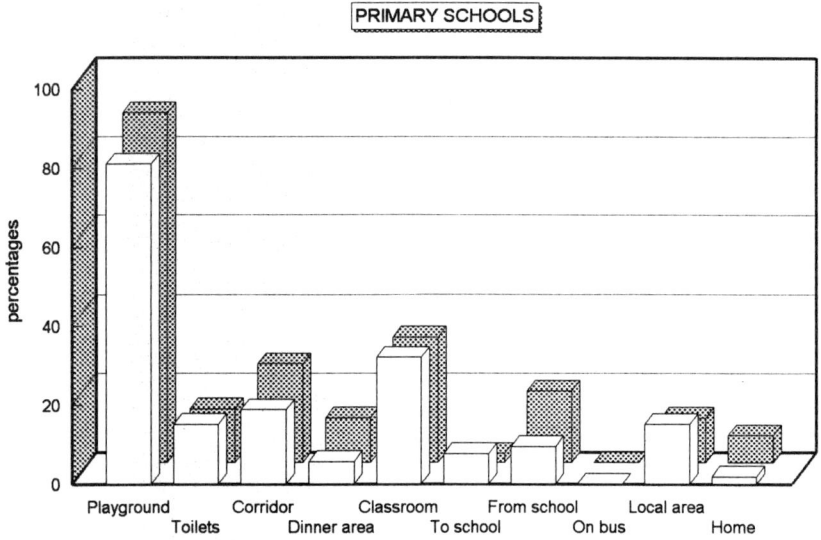

PRIMARY SCHOOLS

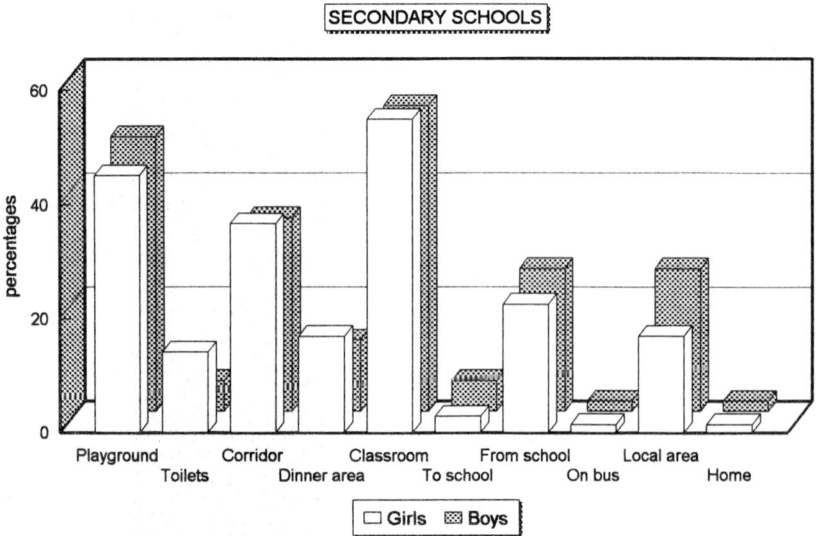

SECONDARY SCHOOLS

□ Girls ▨ Boys

location so percentages do not add up to 100).

Forty-five per cent of the surveyed children indicated that bullying happened in the classroom. Though only four per cent of children calling the Line reported incidents which were clearly happening when staff were present, it is not known what proportion of other children calling the Line and responding to the survey were referring to classroom bullying when a teacher was present.

This is deeply disturbing, particularly as secondary school children cite the classroom as the **most common** bullying location (54%). Surely classroom bullying could be expected to present an opportunity for adult intervention.

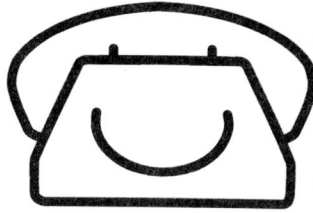

Chapter 6

Who bullies and why?

"I don't want to be a bully but sometimes the opportunity to do something nasty comes up so I do," said Jake, aged 15, who described his bullying as a habit; it made him feel good at the time but horrible afterwards.

Exactly the same picture was presented by Jenny who described getting into the habit through friends' encouragement and finding that it felt good at the time but she felt awful afterwards. Though Jenny was one of only ten callers in the sample who phoned because they were bullying, the 'normality' of this account is borne out by the school survey, where children were very forthcoming about their bullying behaviour. This enabled us to look at who bullies, and why, from the point of view of those bullying and those bullied. Why is a question that perplexes both groups.

Who bullies

Of course, as our school survey clearly demonstrates, the bullies and the bullied are not at all distinct groups of children. Fifteen per cent of the primary sample and 12 per cent of the secondary sample said they had been bullied and had themselves bullied in the past year. So nearly a third of primary school children and nearly a half of secondary school children complaining about having been bullied this year had themselves bullied others.

Table 14 – Surveyed Children
Children who bullied

Primary schools

	Girls	%	Boys	%	Total	%
Ever been bullied	69	62	60	65	129	63
Been a bully	32	29	28	30	60	29
Both bullied and a bully	27	24	23	25	50	24
Been bullied this year	53	47	44	47	97	47
A bully this year	21	19	16	17	37	18
Bullied this year/a bully	17	15	14	15	31	15
Total surveyed	112		93		205	

Secondary schools

	Girls	%	Boys	%	Total	%
Ever been bullied	119	52	98	39	217	45
Been a bully	104	46	102	40	206	43
Both bullied and a bully	71	31	53	21	124	26
Been bullied this year	71	31	56	22	127	26
A bully this year	58	25	61	24	119	25
Bullied this year/a bully	33	14	23	9	56	12
Total surveyed	228		253		481	

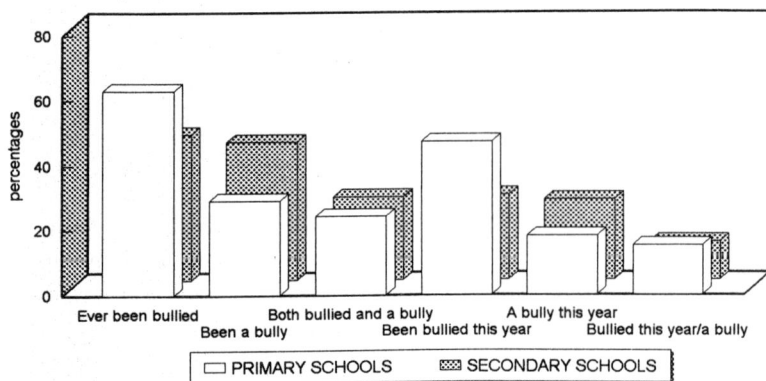

Forty-four per cent of secondary students and 28 per cent of primary school pupils said they had participated in bullying at some point in their school. (See table 14 opposite for a full comparison.) Secondary school children admitted more bullying than primary children. It may be that more bullying in primary schools is done by fewer children; but it seems more likely that secondary children are more able to perceive that what they are doing is bullying and perhaps more prepared to admit to wrongdoing.

The most common form of bullying admitted was name-calling (nearly 80% of children who said they bullied); the least likely to be admitted was physical violence, apart from pushing (12% of primary and 22% of secondary children who bullied). It is possible that much of the physical bullying is done by only a few children, but it is also likely that children are more reluctant to admit to hitting other children than to other forms of bullying.

Bullying by adults

Though the vast majority of children were complaining about bullying by other children, some said adults were responsible. These were mainly adults in their immediate families, with fathers then mothers being most often mentioned. Over the entire Bullying Line, 4.4 per cent of children (188) said they were being bullied by adults, 34 of whom said that a teacher was responsible.

Group bullying

In nearly three quarters of calls to the Line children gave some information about who was bullying them. The majority (73%) reported being bullied by a group of children. This is a higher proportion of group bullying than that reported (65%) on the 1990 Bullying Line. Boys reported slightly more group bullying (76%) than girls (71%).

Not all children surveyed said whether they suffered individual or group bullying. Of those who did, twice as much group as individual bullying was described by secondary school children, a third as much again by primary girls, and the same amount by primary boys. (see table 15 overleaf).

Table 15 – Surveyed Children
Status of children who bullied

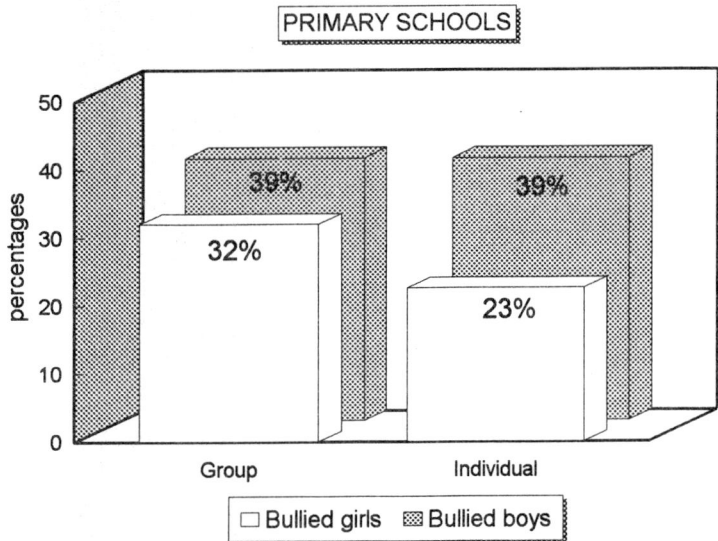

PRIMARY SCHOOLS

percentages

39% | 39%
32%
23%

Group Individual

☐ Bullied girls ▨ Bullied boys

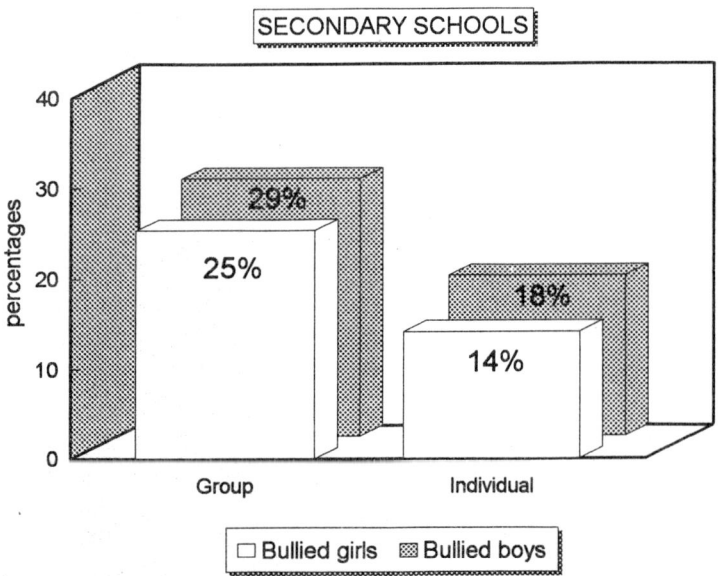

SECONDARY SCHOOLS

percentages

29%
25%
18%
14%

Group Individual

☐ Bullied girls ▨ Bullied boys

Gender of bullies

In 27 per cent of the bullying reported to the Line, there was no data on the gender of the bullies. Where this was reported, most girls were bullied by girls and most boys by boys. Twelve per cent of girls complained of being bullied by boys whereas only 1.4 per cent of boys complained of bullying by girls. Thus, 99 per cent of bullying girls were reported to be bullying children of the same sex, while 41 per cent of male bullies were bullying girls.

The picture from the schools survey is less clear cut. As table 16 shows, surveyed boys and girls in primary and secondary schools described more mixed bullying.

Though these findings confirm previous research (Olweus, 1993) which indicates that boys are more likely to bully since they also bully children of the opposite sex, in the survey 58 per cent of primary and 46 per cent of secondary boys said they were bullied by girls as well as boys, and ten per cent said they were bullied by girls alone.

Girls were slightly more likely to admit to bullying than boys in the survey. This may just mean that they find it easier to admit, but it may indicate that more girls are involved in group bullying or that bullying is done by just as many girls as boys when all forms of bullying are included in the count. Though one 14-year-old male caller was in no doubt:

> *"I am sure that having girls at the school helps to prevent bullying."*

Age of bullies

The age of bullies compared with the victims of bullying has received considerable research attention. The information from the Bullying Line suggests that, although a significant proportion (37%) of bullying followed the established stereotype of older children picking on younger ones, it mainly occurs among peers in the same age group. Fifty-six per cent of callers giving information about age

Table 16 – Surveyed Children
Gender of children who bullied

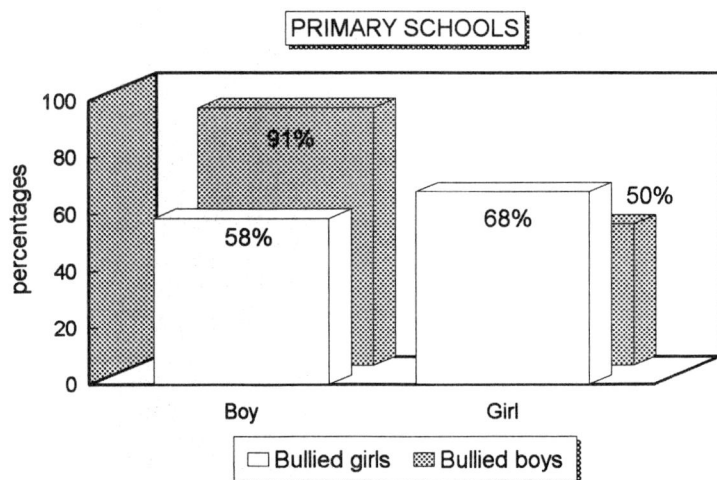

PRIMARY SCHOOLS

percentages

100
80
60
40
20
0

91%

58%

68%

50%

Boy   Girl

☐ Bullied girls   ▨ Bullied boys

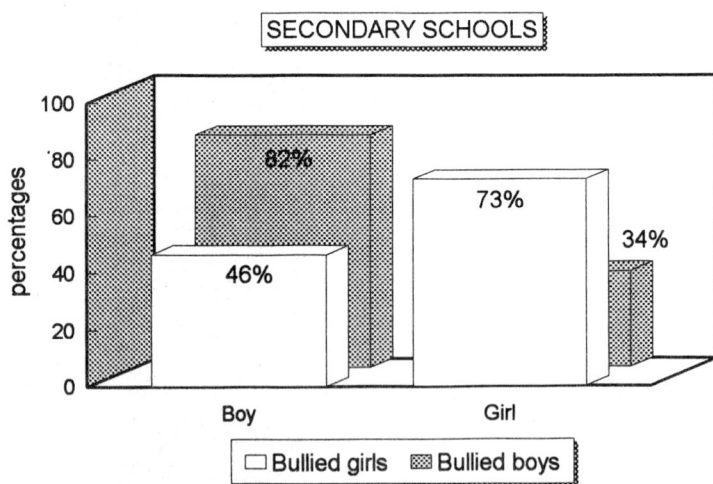

SECONDARY SCHOOLS

percentages

100
80
60
40
20
0

82%

46%

73%

34%

Boy   Girl

☐ Bullied girls   ▨ Bullied boys

indicated that the bullies were the same age as themselves. In less than one per cent of cases were children being bullied by a child younger than themselves. The remainder were being bullied by children of mixed ages.

Information from the survey in schools paints a similar picture. The findings in Table 17 overleaf demonstrate that children understand that age plays some part in who is picked on, and that as children get older, they are more likely to identify children of the same age as the bullies.

Older children in primary schools were very fearful of what would happen to them when they moved up into secondary. They were concerned that the level of bullying might be higher at secondary school, particularly when they first started, since they would be the youngest in the school. As Vikki (13) explained retrospectively:

> *"Well, you're top of the other school and you get here and you're right down at the bottom again and you think, oh no, all the fifth years and all the people above me are going to be really nasty and all the rumours that go round about them picking on you and kicking you and things. You're like, oh I don't want to go, but my brother was here so that helped."*

Evidence from this and other studies does suggest that the transition to secondary school produces an increase in bullying. This may be much more to do with the kind of group behaviour which marks the start of new groups. Bion (1961), the influential group analyst and theorist, described this kind of group as a 'basic assumption' group, where high anxiety levels bring paranoid and persecutory group behaviour, and scapegoating is common. Translating this model to children, it is only too obvious that anxieties about new teachers, friends, work, new environment produce a volatile situation where bullying can easily arise. And when that is placed alongside the particular developmental stage which these children are experiencing with all the emotional uproar which early adolescence involves, it is not surprising that new vulnerabilities emerge to upset individual and group equilibrium.

Table 17 – Surveyed Children
Relative age of children who bullied

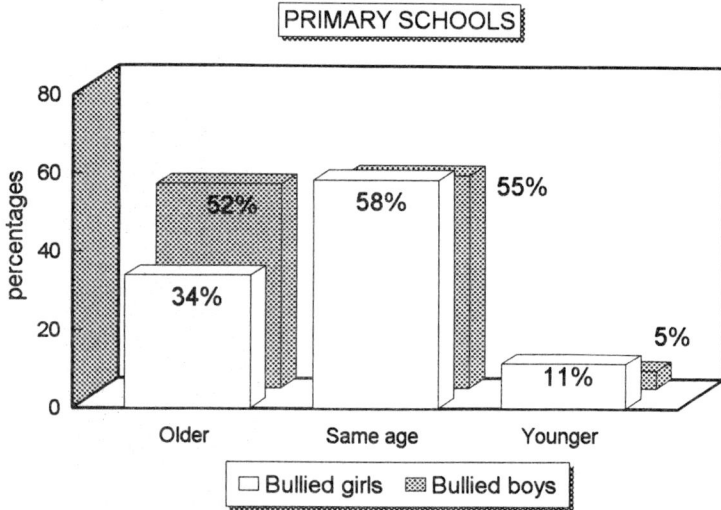

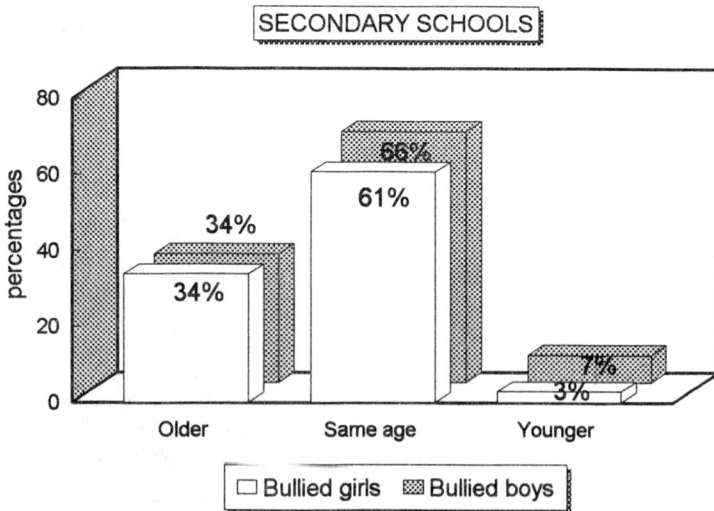

PRIMARY SCHOOLS

percentages

80

60 52% 58% 55%

40 34%

20 5%

11%

0

Older   Same age   Younger

☐ Bullied girls ▨ Bullied boys

SECONDARY SCHOOLS

percentages

80

60 66% 61%

40 34% 34%

20

7%
0 3%

Older   Same age   Younger

☐ Bullied girls ▨ Bullied boys

Supervision and organised support to newcomers at this time from staff and older students is likely to reduce levels and seriousness of bullying considerably.

Why children bully

"I want to stop but I'm scared the ringleaders will turn on me."

"I started so I'd seem 'hard,' so no-one would pick on me. Now it's a habit and I can't stop but I really want to."

"My family deal with arguments by being violent. I need to find other ways to settle arguments."

These statements were made by children calling the Line, asking for help to stop bullying. They focus on habit and learned behaviour. Young people interviewed emphasised taking their feelings out on others as the trigger:

"Probably because I was, like, angry about something and I was taking it out on someone else, I think."

"I've had to push to protect myself from bullying sometimes."

A large proportion of children calling the Line because of being bullied wanted to understand why they were being picked on by bullies. Many were aware of a superficial reason - the name they were being called or what the bully said or did to them was indicative. However, during counselling, children often talked of their feeling that they possessed some unknown characteristic or had done something which had made the bullies pick on them.

Indeed, the response of parents and staff approached for help by children often reinforced the child's worries in this respect. Adults were reported to have asked children such questions as 'How did all this start?' 'What did you do to them to bring this on?' and 'People don't pick on you for no reason' when told of the bullying.

The view that certain children may incite or cause bullies to pick on them is prevalent in the literature on bullying and, from what bullied children say, is a common view among teachers. Pikas (1989) identified 'provocative victims' - children whose behaviour annoys other children and who 'provoke' exasperated responses. Following this theme, a range of anti-bullying strategies have been developed which focus on helping the child to make specific responses to the bully to deter or prevent further abuse. While bullied children may indeed benefit enormously from social skills training or counselling, it is all too easy for adults and other children to see the nastiness as in some way justified, and to fall into blaming the victims rather than tackling the bullying.

The experience of being bullied in itself can lead to emotional and educational difficulties (Olweus 1995, Farrington 1993) which may be wrongly seen as a cause rather than a consequence. Some children calling the Line revealed longstanding behaviour difficulties, some saying very frankly that they tended to annoy other children. But a victim approach essentially fails to address the complexity of the problem - a particular child or children may be singled out for any number of reasons or purely arbitrarily.

In similar vein, a great deal of research on bullying has focused on the individual characteristics of children who bully, linking bullying behaviour to family difficulties, and to aggressive/impulsive tendencies which can be identified early in a child's history.

The picture described by children themselves is less clear cut and more complex. The fact that over 70 per cent of bullying complained of is group bullying means that causes have to be sought in the way groups organise themselves as well as in individual children's characteristics. Far too little attention has been spent developing understanding of the dynamics of children's groups; how groups change with changing circumstances; and how their structures are influenced by social and cultural factors. The very fact that whole-school programmes have been shown to reduce the seriousness and incidence of bullying in schools demonstrates that the culture of a school is an appropriate central focus for anti-bullying action.

Some group bullying may be orchestrated by a particular individual in the group; but searching for individual children's 'pathology' offers only limited help in understanding bullying.

Though little benefit comes from seeking the answer to the question 'Why do children bully?' in individual children's characteristics, asking children themselves is illuminating. Children answer the question differently depending on whether they are talking about themselves or other children.

Children who bully talk about opportunity, habit, pleasure, followed by remorse. Those surveyed who said they had bullied (23% of the sample) usually offered more than one explanation but mainly ascribed the bullying to their feelings, largely anger (52%) or jealousy. Bullying for 'entertainment' came next - those who bullied for fun or because they were bored (30%). A few children said they had bullied following arguments or rows. Interestingly, none of them singled out their own or the victim's individual characteristics as an explanation, though 'not liking' featured.

A different picture was presented by the responses from the whole sample to the general question, 'Why do children bully in school?' Though taking feelings out on others (62%), arguments and 'entertainment' were prominent, there was also frequent mention of individual characteristics of the bullied child which drew the fire, and 'psychological' motivations of bullies: to show off or be powerful (the most common explanation), because they were bullied themselves or had an unhappy home. As Lisa (14) explained:

> *"They think it makes 'em higher or bigger than anyone else, they think they're better than anyone else. Or they might know someone who bullies and, thinking they're hard and all that, they start doing it themselves to make 'em think they're a bit hard, you know, like mates."*

In similar vein, Max, aged ten, linked having been bullied to the need to establish power and status with other children, especially for boys, and the importance of demonstrating it.

"'cause they got bullied when they were younger. They think they are strong and hard. Boys do it more 'cause boys think they're stronger and can do anything."

Children aged seven and under who were interviewed often simply speculated that children bullied people 'because they didn't like them'. This has to be considered seriously. Many children, like adults, consider that not liking somebody gives them a licence to be nasty to him or her. How nasty nasty is depends partly on individual characteristics of the child, but also on group norms and on school and family culture. And it is the group which legitimises the behaviour and promotes it.

Most respondents and callers gave a variety of reasons for bullying, including family problems, being bullied themselves and wanting to take it out on someone else, mimicking other children/adults who were bullies, or getting in with the wrong crowd or gang who made a habit of bullying. They demonstrated that they understood clearly that bullying behaviour has many origins. Charlotte (15) illustrated this:

"It could be problems at home, they could be taking their feelings out on someone, they could just do it for fun 'cause they think they're big, or they've just got nothing else to do."

Labelling or categorising according to temperaments or personal characteristics oversimplifies the origins of bullying behaviour. This in turn limits thinking about how to intervene, and reduces, for bullying and bullied children, their capacity to free themselves from the effects of bullying.

It is absolutely clear, then, that strategies for dealing with bullying have to focus on group behaviour - staff understanding the dynamics of children's groups and learning how to deploy group skills. In neither call nor school sample did children provide evidence of group techniques being used routinely to handle incidents, despite all the practical advice available to schools.

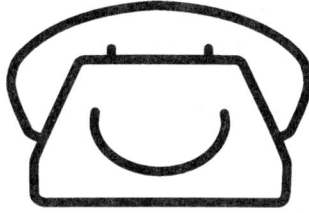

Chapter 7

The effects and consequences of bullying

"If I told anyone they would not believe me."

"I can't stop thinking about it. I want to move schools but Mum said that might not help and it would happen again."

"I don't know why but I can't stand up to them even though I know karate. It feels as bad as when my parents got divorced."

"I cry every day. I feel so bad. The teacher said I set it off myself."

Children's accounts of bullying, both on the Line, and when interviewed in the school survey, emphasised the effects of bullying, particularly feelings of misery, powerlessness and hopelessness. Harjeet (13) explained during interview how he felt at school when he was called racist names by a group of boys in his year:

"It felt horrible, I felt scared to come to school. I felt relieved that I would have different lessons to them sometimes, otherwise I'd just sit away from them across the class or something and try not to attract their attention."

Children commonly reported feeling isolated, frightened, sad, and in some cases angry about the treatment they received from bullies, but also preoccupied by it. They could not get it out of their minds. Others talked about **very** long-term effects:

> *"It took me a long time to get my confidence back - years, really. I still think about it and get upset."*

For many children these feelings spilt over into their relationships with others and inhibited their ability to function properly. Relationships with parents and siblings were often the first to be affected, especially for those children who felt powerless to stop the bullying and unable to share their problems with others. Kathy, a 12-year-old girl, described how she felt when she was being bullied:

> *"Now I am happier. I get on with my parents really well, but when all this was going on with Claire, I really turned badly against my mum and dad. I couldn't do anything about it (the bullying) at school so I did it at home."*

The most common effect described to counsellors by child callers was on their emotional state. The majority of callers were preoccupied by feelings of sadness and misery and a third of the callers talked about the depth of their fear of the bullies. Other children described themselves as 'depressed', 'anxious', 'really low'. The shame and humiliation involved in being bullied and not being able to do anything about it were mentioned again and again. This contributed both to the difficulty some children had in telling others what was happening and to the effect the bullying had on their self- esteem.

Others reported their reluctance to go to school; some had pretended to be ill to avoid going; a small group had resorted to truancy; and some were considering injuring themselves. Some suffered headaches and stomach aches or increasing asthma attacks. Fifteen per cent specifically reported that their school work had been affected.

Suicidal feelings and attempts

"Recently I've started thinking about killing myself. I feel too scared to have a social life. I spend my days in fear in and out of school."

This is how Jill (13) described her state of mind after months of daily name-calling and threats to beat her up. Her friend from infant school who now went to school elsewhere had been provoking children at Jill's school to gang up against her. Her parents had been to the school several times to try to resolve the problems, but they had not been able to see the headteacher. The school liaison officer had told her mother that she felt she should keep Jill off school for a time.

Jill was one of a small but significant group (4% - 62 children) who discussed suicidal feelings or attempted suicide with counsellors. A further seven children were identified as feeling suicidal by other children calling on their behalf, and two parents called, having found their sons actively trying to kill themselves by hanging. Suicidal thoughts and attempts were more frequently described by boys - seven per cent of all boys calling the Bullying Line compared with four per cent of girls. Considering that there has been a dramatic increase in suicides among young males, *Trust for the Study of Adolescence* (1995), and that older boys do seem to have difficulty in reporting bullying and asking for help, this is extremely worrying.

Most of the children feeling suicidal had been bullied for some time, though five had been bullied for a relatively short period (less than a month).

It is important to note that these cases were not confined to particularly brutal or physical bullying actions. Over half (52%) of the children were experiencing exclusively verbal forms of abuse, most commonly name-calling. Rejection, humiliation and vilification are experienced as an attack on a child's sense of self. As one girl said from boarding school: "I think mental bullying is worse." It is extremely difficult to go on believing you are lovable and worthwhile under a barrage of this kind of harassment.

The effects and consequences of bullying can devastate a child's life and in some cases lead to suicide. Several child suicides each year have been linked to bullying, Smith and Sharp (1995); and reported cases are not confined to children experiencing physical attacks, but also children suffering verbal bullying. The cases of children who reported feeling suicidal and/or attempting suicide suggest that it is dangerous to label some forms of bullying as 'mild' bullying. Instances of bullying dismissed by adults as trivial can fundamentally undermine a child's sense of well-being and self-esteem.

Since there is no sure way of identifying children who may react in a self-destructive way to different types of bullying, the onus must be on adults to listen to, and be guided by the child's expressed thoughts and feelings, rather than by any preconceived ideas about the relative severity of different forms of bullying.

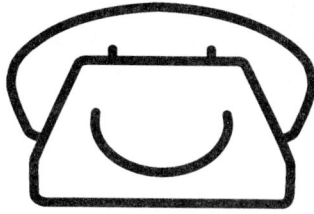

Chapter 8

Asking for help

"I suppose this school does try to do things but they don't tell you what they're going to do enough. So if people are getting bullied, they don't want to go tell teachers 'cause they don't know what they're going to do." (Augustin (14) during interview)

"I saw a small boy being bullied by a gang in the park. They swore at him and kicked him. I was too scared to do anything in case they turned on me." (Duncan, aged 13, who was ringing for help because of being bullied himself.)

It is commonly believed that children do not get help when they are being bullied because they do not ask for it - they are unable to talk about what is happening to them. Seventeen per cent of the children calling the Line, and 14% of the caller sample, were in that position. However, the evidence from this study and our previous work on bullying is that most children do ask for help and do so repeatedly from adults and other children, despite threats from bullying children, shame, and fear of the consequences. The majority of child callers had told and were ringing about bullying which persisted despite adults' attempts to help. The picture from the survey was rather better, in that the bullying children complained of was less grave, of shorter duration, and, having told, they were more likely to experience a positive outcome. These schools were, of course, alive to the problem of bullying and all had made moves to tackle it. Yet, here too, many children talked of bullying which persisted despite their having told. The question posed by their experience is why? Why is it so difficult to stop the bullying of an individual child? Children's accounts of what happens when they do tell give us some of the answers.

Children who don't tell

"The boys have sworn to get back at me. They said they would kill me," said Chris, 11, about the consequences of telling.

Some children (17%) calling had not told anyone else about their bullying, boys more commonly than girls. Although the full range of bullying behaviour was represented, those who were being subjected to extortion were more likely to have told no-one - over a third (38%) of the 75 children whose main problem was having their money/possessions taken by force. Children in the school survey presented a similar picture. One 11-year-old girl caller told of having had her lunch taken away almost daily for a year and not being able to tell.

It is possible that children having their things taken are subject to greater intimidation or feelings of humiliation, and that children who steal and extort are more practised at terrorising their targets into submission.

Younger children expressed very few reservations about telling, but as children get older, it seems that they may well fear severe consequences if they tell. Children had been threatened that if they told a member of staff about the bullying, they would be beaten up outside school or bullied in some other way. During interview boys over 14 were most likely to raise concerns about the consequences of telling.

Children who tell

The overwhelming majority of callers about whom we have data (82%) and of children taking part in the schools survey (84%) had told someone about the bullying. Most had told more than one person (70% of primary and 50% of secondary respondents).

In the school survey, primary children were most likely to tell (90%), with boys slightly more likely to do so than girls. Older children were somewhat less likely to tell (77%) and older boys **most** likely not to have told (33% of older boys compared with 15% of girls). While 68 per cent of primary children who had told someone had told school staff, fewer secondary children (40%) had done so. They were more likely to tell friends.

As table 18 overleaf demonstrates, staff in schools were the most likely confidants of children in the survey; 70 per cent of the children who had previously discussed their problem had told a member of staff. Children were less likely to have told their parents (58%). The call sample, on the contrary, were more likely to have told parents than school staff. It is tempting to speculate that children tell their teachers in schools which are sympathetic to the bullied child's plight, but tell their parents when schools are not, so that parents contacting these schools on their children's behalf are also likely to receive a cursory response.

Friends had been approached for support by 14 per cent of children using the Line and 50 per cent of those in the school sample.

These findings reflect a considerable improvement on the situation reported by Whitney and Smith (1993). Their schools' survey showed that half the incidents of bullying had been reported to no-one. While ChildLine's research showed that children are generally willing to tell people about a problem of bullying, it must be remembered that the children surveyed attended schools which openly acknowledged that bullying happened. However, recent research in Tower Hamlets (1995) confirms that most children tell about bullying.

Table 18 – Who children told about a bullying problem

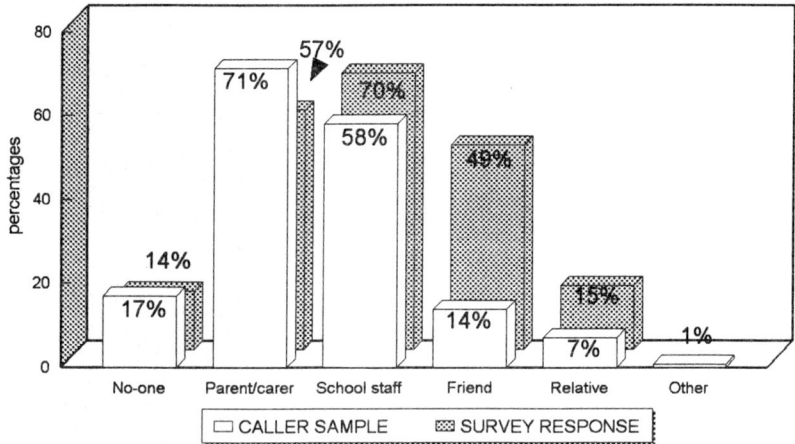

What happened when children told

Although some of the actions taken by adults had been perceived as supportive by the child at the time they were taken, the information from the call sample about what happens when adults are told is not encouraging. Overall 57 per cent (267) of children who had told their parents about the problem had experienced no change or a negative outcome as a result of telling. Seventy-two per cent (174 children) of those cases where a parent or main carer had spoken to the school resulted in a continuation or worsening of the problem. Actions initiated by school staff themselves fared better, only 28 per cent of children who had told their schools specifically reporting that their actions had simply not helped or worsened the situation.

In most of these cases (69%), then, adult interventions had been ineffective or counter-productive. Of course, the Bullying Line was likely to hear from those children who had not been helped. Yet their accounts can help us to understand why so many adult interventions do not help the child and, in turn, how they can be made more effective.

Their accounts revealed three general adult responses to being told about bullying, and a similar pattern emerges from the questionnaire and interviews:

- a refusal to accept the seriousness of the problem for the child;
- taking peremptory action on behalf of the child ; or
- suggesting that the child has to sort it out for himself/herself.

Ignoring or denying the problem

Ten per cent of children calling the Bullying Line and 19 per cent of those surveyed in schools reported that when they had told about a bullying problem, adults had not accepted it and refused to act to help them. A range of practical issues, possibly not having time to listen, may play a part when an adult refuses to accept, believe or respond to a child reporting bullying. But so does the commonly held belief that bullying is a minor problem - an inevitable part of growing up, something all children have to face as they go through school, and that children who cannot shrug it off are the problem rather than the bullying itself. As one parent wrote:

"Perhaps it would be better to concentrate on the worse forms of bullying and hopefully stamp them out, but teasing, name-calling, excluding from games and spreading rumours are not what I would call bullying, they have always happened and always will."

Staff in schools were commonly described as having denied that there **was** a problem of bullying, either by blaming the bullied child, saying they provoked the other children or were over-sensitive to comments made by them, or suggesting that parents were being over-protective and refusing to let their child come to terms with everyday interactions with other children. If a child or parents kept on complaining, **they** would begin to be dealt with as the problem, much to their distress.

William was 10 years old and had been teased relentlessly about his weight for three years. He told ChildLine that he tried to diet, but could not lose weight. He had told the school and they had suggested he try to ignore it. He was now feeling so desperate about facing the teasing at school that he was thinking of killing himself. "I wish I could go to sleep and never wake up," he said. In this instance, with William's agreement, ChildLine phoned the school who had not understood until then how very depressed he was.

It appears to be difficult for teachers and for parents to recognise when children are driven beyond their endurance, particularly when the problem is 'just' teasing. Of course, some children who become targets do require help with specific problems, including some aspects of their own behaviour. This help can be provided alongside steps to put a stop to the bullying

Taking action for the child

Most adults (62% of those on the Line) were reported to have responded by 'taking over'. They were very concerned about the child and did this with the best of intentions, aiming to put things right for the child.

Nearly 500 children from the call sample had told their parents. Most parents had then gone to the school to talk to a member of staff - 55 per cent of parents did this immediately. The parents of some 12 per cent of children had straightaway approached the parents of the bully. In all these cases the bullying persisted despite the actions taken.

Parents naturally feel strongly about their child being bullied and want to do something about it as quickly as possible. But in their desire to act to protect their child they leave him or her out of their actions and decisions.

Staff in schools may take the problem out of the child's hands for different reasons, perhaps because they may have a number of competing demands which make it difficult to seek out the individual child's needs and wishes; or they may believe that their interventions will invariably be effective because of their position of authority in the school; or they may consider this is the right thing to do and what is expected of them.

Staff were most likely to reprimand or punish the bullying child or children or to approach the bully's parent either to discuss the problem or to punish the bully. Of the two, punishment was more frequently reported on the Line. Bullies had been given detentions, denied privileges, sent to see the headteacher, told off and had letters sent to their parents. A very small proportion (less than 1%) had been excluded from the school for their behaviour. There was little evidence that any of the group strategies for tackling bullying were ever considered or used.

Bullied children described feeling cut off from the decision-making process after having told. Adults would decide unilaterally what action to take without seeking the views of the child about their intentions, or only afterwards tell them what they had done. Staff would commonly tell children that they would 'sort the problem out', but most children were left not knowing what they would do or had done.

Let the child resolve it

On the Line children reported that adults had told them to 'ignore' or 'avoid the bully' or 'fight back'. Advice to ignore the bullying was the most common of these. A quarter of children who had told their parents about bullying had been told to ignore the bullies; a smaller proportion (9%) had been given similar advice from staff in schools. A much smaller group had been told to stick up for themselves or fight back against the bully. All these responses put the onus on the **children** to resolve the problem entirely themselves. But as Sue (13) explained during interview:

> *"It is difficult to ignore people that have been calling you names. Like you think, I'm going to ignore them completely, I'm not going to listen to anything they say, but like when you come home from school you might just let it all out and cry and everything. But I don't think you could ever really ignore what they've been saying. You might feel as if you are, at school, but when you get home and realise and think over what they've been saying you can just let it all out then, sort of thing. Especially if it goes*

*on continuously, you know like every time he or she walks
past you and says something, it is difficult to ignore, 'cause
you know they're saying that directly to you and not other
people."*

Other adults had offered children advice on strategies to avoid the
bullying: for example, to stay close to their friends at those times
of the day when they were normally picked on. Schools were also
reported to have told children to stay in at break times to avoid the
bullies; others had moved the bullied child into another class in the
hope that they could avoid the problem. Unfortunately, the children
ringing ChildLine had not found these actions put a stop to the
bullying; indeed some found that avoidance had drawn attention to
them, and children told counsellors that the bullies had simply
found other times or places to bully them.

Helping the bullied child

ChildLine hears from some children and young people who feel driven
by being bullied into taking the law into their own hands. This can
turn out very badly - and not just for the bully. As one boy, who
was expelled for hitting and kicking the boy who had bullied him,
put it,

"This has turned me into a bully too."

But it is all very well for people outside the situation to say this is
not a sensible thing to do; it is quite another to know how to handle
it when you are being bullied. Children commonly feel nothing
they can do can change things. Bullies succeed because they are
frightening or they gang up on children. So being brave and
standing up for yourself is much easier said than done. And all the
young people who ring ChildLine say it's no good to be told to
ignore it. They are upset and frightened - sometimes terrified -
and they can't stop thinking about it. We asked children in the
survey what could be done to help.

Putting a stop to the bullying was of course felt to be most important, but there was little awareness of approaches other than sanctions or punishments. Most children felt uncertain about how best to intervene to stop bullying though they wanted to be able to do so.

According to the children studied here, there was startlingly little use made of the inventive ideas about tackling bullying outlined for schools in a plethora of recent guidance, some even mailed out to schools. Group techniques like the 'No blame' approach or 'Method of shared concern' were not mentioned, nor were bully lines, bully boxes, peer counselling, mentoring or mediation schemes. These approaches simply do not appear to be part of the repertoire of many schools. Nor did they appear to be widely known by parents, staff or children in the survey.

All these groups understood the impact bullying has on children's emotional state and felt this too should be tackled, but again without real confidence that they knew how to help. Children talked of being friendly to a child who had been bullied, or taking a bullied child to a member of staff for support:

> *"Someone should talk to them and reassure them and cheer them up really, 'cause when they're upset the bullies will sort of see that," said Paul, aged 14.*

Many of the older children felt it was important to reassure bullied children that it was not their fault that they had been bullied and to let them talk it through. Parents and staff felt it was important to build up children's confidence. Some staff felt that children might need to practise being more assertive, so that they did not become a 'victim' again.

Children calling the Bullying Line were anxious both to discuss with counsellors their feelings about the bullying and the effects it was having on them, **and** to explore possible ways of resolving the problem. They did present, on the whole, a picture of their feelings having been readily disregarded or dismissed. Though most children had found they could tell the adults in their lives about the bullying, it was much harder to disclose the level of their distress, anguish and fear. Of course, this demonstrates that both action to stop bullying, **and** emotional support, are necessary in moving towards a resolution, and the suggestions in the final section of this book have been developed on this basis.

Chapter 9

School strategies and responses to them

The Department for Education has in recent years put its weight behind the view that schools must assume responsibility for tackling bullying. In 1992, the Scottish Council for Research in Education anti-bullying pack was circulated to schools. Departmental guidance on inspections requires school inspectors to investigate schools' handling of bullying as part of any school inspection. In 1994 the Department for Education pack, *Don't suffer in silence*, based on the Sheffield University action research in primary and secondary schools, was made available to schools. The pack recommends that schools define and develop behaviour policies and anti-bullying strategies as part of a 'whole school' approach to tackling bullying.

All four schools studied by ChildLine were following this advice. Three had policies in place, while the fourth school was on the verge of producing one. The schools were open to accepting that bullying happened and the policies (simpler and more comprehensive) encouraged children to tell, and promised children and adults a sympathetic hearing. Across all the schools 90 per cent of children surveyed responded that teachers and staff talked about bullying. And, certainly, children in all schools wrote and talked about being bullied and bullying very openly. More children in these schools were willing to admit to bullying than in previous surveys.

Those children who had experienced bullying in the schools survey presented a much less grave picture than those phoning the Bullying Line. They expected to be able to tell, there was less physical bullying reported, bullying which **had** occurred was of much shorter duration, and children reported a better outcome from telling adults. So these four schools have much to be pleased about. But, even there, in schools with a real acknowledgement of the importance of dealing with bullying, there were children who could not get effective help, and there was little evidence of the use of group approaches. Children, parents and staff were not complacent or completely satisfied with the state of anti-bullying work in all schools. They had many suggestions about how to improve matters further and these are outlined below. As Emily (16) explained during interview when asked if she thought the code helped prevent bullying:

> *"It (the code of conduct) does in some ways, but it goes out of your head. The first years when they come in, they'll know it and they'll stick to it. But as you get older you forget about the code of conduct, you don't even know it's there half the time. You get told it once a year about, it's on all the doors but you don't really look at it."*

This case study is too limited by far to make any confident comparisons between the schools. As Farrington has indicated, we are a long way from having a research model which allows us to identify and compare all the factors - individual, family, societal and organisational - which together determine the patterns of bullying and response in schools (Farrington 1993).

Yet it was noticeable from the schools' survey that children at one of the schools, Sandwell Middle School, displayed more confidence in their school's capacity to tackle bullying problems. And this particular school seemed to have gone further in moving from policy and principle into practice.

For though a statement of expectations is important in laying out what is and is not acceptable, it does not seem on its own to affect the way children actually behave, even assuming that they can remember what it says. The responses from children at Sandwell Middle school, however, suggest that when staff and parents actively adopt a model of behaviour which demonstrates what is expected of the children, this helps establish a sounder practice - encouraging good behaviour by example as well as precept.

Sandwell children demonstrated a more comprehensive understanding of the bullies' motivations and recognised that they too might have unresolved problems and need for support. They were also more likely to suggest positive responses to bullying behaviour like 'try and talk to them' or 'try and make friends with them' rather than only punitive responses.

Much cannot be concluded from any comparison of the incidence of bullying across the schools since two were primary and two secondary, and their catchment areas were different. However, the form and duration of bullying incidents in Sandwell school were different, involving mainly verbal forms of bullying (49% in questionnaire and 61% during interviews) about which children were very willing to tell staff and parents. Furthermore, the duration of bullying incidents was relatively short: 44 per cent lasted less than a week. Bullying incidents, once reported, had a good chance of being resolved. From the 79 cases where information on the outcome of the bullying was available, nearly half (49% - 39 children) reported an effective resolution. Interviews confirmed the confidence Sandwell children expressed in the survey about involving adults in the resolution of bullying problems.

Children's views and suggestions

Children in schools were asked what they thought would be helpful to stop bullying. They had suggestions covering all aspects of anti-bullying work, coming up with many of the same ideas as those in the anti-bullying packs. Their responses support a broad school approach.

- They appreciated structured opportunities for raising and discussing bullying and its effects - schools which had initiated drama or English exercises on bullying issues had been found particularly helpful.

- They highlighted the importance of receiving a positive response from people they told about bullying so that confidence develops across the entire school.

- They emphasised throughout the study the importance of being included and participating in the handling of bullying incidents. A 15-year-old suggested: *"Kids could set up a school bullying committee and try and talk about what they could do, and try to get everyone to see that bullying isn't the thing to do."*

- They saw the importance of a 'culture of decency' - the school promoting positive social behaviour among children and with adults. Seventeen per cent of children specifically said that being kinder and more respectful of each other's needs and feelings were important ways of helping to prevent bullying.

- They understood - without putting it explicitly - the role of the bystander. They wished to be better equipped through discussion and practice to help children who were being bullied. Over half (57%) of the children in the survey said they would like to be able to offer help and assistance to other children they saw being bullied but most (45%) were unsure what they could actually do to be helpful, and ended up mostly doing nothing.

- When it came to dealing with bullies, children tended to emphasise the pattern in their schools, with 54 per cent indicating that punishment was the answer. However, children thought that parents should be much more involved in the punishment: *"because,"* said a ten year old girl, *"if they thought they would get done by parents they would bully less, 'cause parents can stop pocket money, ground kids, and it's more effective than teachers."*

- A quarter thought parents should discuss the problem of bullying more with their children and 15 per cent felt staff should provide more opportunities for discussion of the issue in school. As one girl said: *"Just telling them off and punishing them doesn't work. They need to really talk about it and think what it feels like."* Again, without explicitly putting it into words, children appreciate the necessity for 'talking' approaches to prevention and management of incidents of bullying.

- Closer supervision of children and playgrounds especially at break times was mentioned by 14 per cent of children. Others suggested that different areas of the playground should be designated for different age groups.

Staff suggestions

"Each case must be dealt with individually. Different people bully for different reasons, and how they should be dealt with is dependent on why they bully. To help the bully you need to understand them so you can give them the right support. You can't just say, 'It's wrong, don't do it'. (A female member of staff)

The small group of staff who responded to the survey (46) made a range of suggestions, echoing many of the children's:

• closer supervision of children in schools;

• more opportunities to discuss bullying and children's feelings of vulnerability;

• developing a process for dealing with bullying when it first happens;

• being generally more available to talk to children.

Staff, like children, thought parents could help prevent and stop bullying by being supportive of their child's concerns, talking to them about bullying, and demonstrating to their children that bullying behaviour was not acceptable. They thought that some children who had been bullied might benefit from social skills training, which focused on how to respond to and diffuse bullying behaviour and other difficult situations. The most important single thing noted was for children to feel able to tell staff about the bullying and to rely on the latter to act on their reports. There was, however, no reference to children's need to be involved in the process of handling bullying incidents. Children appeared to be seen as recipients of help rather than participants. Group techniques were not mentioned, though interestingly, several staff thought themselves ill-equipped to respond to the range of issues presented to them as bullying, emphasising the need for staff training in this area.

Parents' suggestions

Parents' responses added to the picture of a broad consensus among adults and children on what could prevent or help stop bullying.

- Three-quarters of respondents thought children should be made more aware of bullying and its consequences through 'educative' approaches.

- Over a quarter emphasised the importance of a culture where children were listened to and encouraged to share their problems.

- Twenty six per cent suggested teaching children social skills at home and in school would reduce the likelihood of their either becoming a bully or being bullied.

- Children should be encouraged to ensure that they involved adults when they themselves were being bullied and/or when they saw others being bullied.

- A quarter of those who responded said they felt children should try to be respectful to each other and be aware of the feelings of other children as a way of reducing bullying.

- A small group (11%) talked about becoming involved in their children's school and supporting their actions as offering a strong united message to children.

- Only seven per cent were in favour of a more punitive approach from the parents of the bully to their child.

However, when asked what they would do if their own child was being bullied, parents' responses were more punitive and less open to children's concerns. Verbal bullying like teasing and name-calling was considered by the majority of parents to be something children should deal with themselves. Most felt threats and physical bullying warranted their intervention. They looked for immediate action from staff as soon as they were aware of it. They wanted those involved to be informed about the consequences and impact of bullying behaviour. Sixteen per cent wanted staff to punish bullying children and thought punishments for bullying should be more severe. Parents did not make much mention of anti-bullying strategies and tended to view bullying as something which other people's children did.

So overall there was a consensus that bullying should be tackled in schools and plenty of shared ideas about how matters, even in these schools, could be improved. But there was a lack of confidence in the actual practice. This is not surprising since bullying is not easy to unravel. It requires persistence, time, and the use of a range of flexible approaches. Sandwell school showed that the way adults behave towards each other and the children in the school is the starting point for any behaviour policy which aims to challenge bullying behaviour and establish a no-bullying culture. On this foundation can be built security and comfort for suffering children through the development of confident anti-bullying practice.

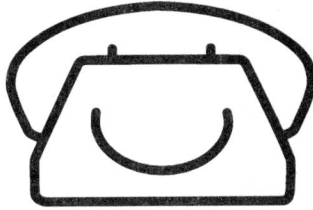

Chapter 10

Conclusions: the messages from the children

The findings of this research indicate that bullying behaviour is complex. Like much aggressive behaviour, it is not susceptible to simple explanation or simple remedies.

It is not even a simple matter to **define** bullying, since children define actions as bullying depending on the feelings and effects the actions of others have on them, and these vary; and adults focus on 'severity', duration, frequency and motivation. The very term 'bullying' is a euphemism for assaults which adults would describe as harassment, verbal abuse, actual or grievous bodily harm, theft, intimidation, extortion, blackmail, sexual or racial harassment, sexual assault, and, occasionally, attempted murder - criminal offences in the adult world.

Neither is there any simple way of gauging or predicting the likely effects or seriousness of bullying on individual children. Individual children describe a wide variety of reactions to very similar events. The effects may pass quickly or they may fundamentally undermine a child's self-esteem, their relations with others and their feelings about school, in extreme cases leading to despair and suicide. Some children, because of positive life experiences, the strength of their own internal resources, the support of peers or the particular form of bullying they receive, do manage to protect themselves in some bullying situations and develop strategies which can diffuse or challenge acts of bullying. Others are thrown into fear or despair, powerless to defend themselves. And there are very few children who can stand up to persistent scapegoating, intimidation or violent assault.

Similarly children get involved in bullying others for various reasons - thoughtlessly, as part of a group process, as a way of taking out their bad feelings on others, to feel tougher and more in control when they are insecure, or to satisfy quite sadistic drives. Some will bully occasionally, whereas others become habitual bullies who require the satisfaction of hurting others. Though research has sought to identify both resilience and risk factors from the study of bullied and bullying children, we are not yet in the state where our knowledge allows certainty in identifying who is at risk and who can be resilient.

These findings pose a considerable challenge to any adult attempting to help children who are being bullied or involved in bullying behaviour. For since the nature of the problem is complex, it is impossible to have a single prescriptive response applicable to all situations.

What we hear from children and adults on the phones and through questionnaires and interviews confirms that the response to individual reports of bullying should be flexible enough to meet the particular circumstances of the children concerned, but at the same time relate to a consistent set of principles and a structure which ensures that matters receive prompt, appropriate attention and follow-up.

But according to children this is not the response they usually receive. Adults are reported to be all too ready to apply a quick fit judgement to the situation and respond in ways which may have little effect on the problem, indeed may actually make it worse.

Children find that many adults dismiss or minimise verbal bullying. Most are much more willing to accept the need for intervention where threats of, or actual physical bullying are involved. Yet children not only find verbal bullying in itself acutely painful, they believe it carries the threat of physical attack or more serious forms of bullying. They commonly describe verbal abuse as **starting** the **process** of bullying.

If children's reading of the situation is right, then more attentive responses to verbal bullying may be the best prevention strategy, helping to avoid the descent into vicious victimisation which children complain of and fear.

The study showed disappointingly little evidence that the wealth of guidance on anti-bullying strategies is bearing fruit in schools. It is hard to escape the conclusion that most books and packs are gathering dust on school shelves. Since 70 per cent of bullying complained of is done by groups of children, techniques like the **method of common concern** and the **no blame approach** should be part of the repertoire of all teachers. Peer counselling and mediation are also reported by children (Thornton, 1993) to be highly effective in reducing bullying, though costly in staff time for training, support, and supervision of students. Some schools establish a member of staff with the responsibility for overseeing and bringing forward the school's anti-bullying work. The responsible staff member can build up knowledge and expertise in techniques for handling individual occurrences and whole school approaches. They can then train other school staff and be available to staff for consultation. Such an approach only works if the whole school community supports the idea. One of the schools studied here had an approach to discipline in which the behaviour of adults served as a role model. Though the limitations of the study prevent definitive statements about the differing school environments, children, parents and teachers from that school did suggest the picture of a school which was getting it right.

An environment which explicitly teaches, by adult example as well as precept, the value of respect for each other's concerns, beliefs and feelings, appears more conducive to a successful resolution of the range of bullying problems than those resting exclusively on a punitive response to the bully.

One of the most dispiriting approaches to bullying behaviour is viewing it as a 'natural' part of childhood and school life: it has always been there, always will be there and therefore, from the

Olympian detachment of adulthood, it is best not fussed about. No sensible person would suggest that a high prevalence rate for any illness from influenza to cancer should be an argument for doing nothing about it; nor that an illness seen in each generation and never entirely stamped out, should require no focus of attention in attempting to reduce or prevent as much of it as is possible.

This study, like others, shows that bullying is a common experience for children, that it is a continuing problem with each cohort of children, and that we do not yet know enough to be able to eliminate it. But it also does show that some interventions are more effective than others, that some do reduce the seriousness and duration of incidents, and the number of children affected by serious assaults. Most of all it shows that those children and young people affected by bullying want it to be tackled. They do want to have a fuss made. It is time to view bullying as a disease in schools and on the streets and to adopt a nationwide strategy to tackle it, using the strategies and techniques already tested and found to be effective.

In this, the relationship between staff in schools, children and parents is clearly crucial. Many parents feel reluctant to approach the school repeatedly about their child's bullying problem in case they themselves become identified as the problem. Schools should endeavour to foster relationships with parents which allow them opportunities to raise their fears and concerns for their child's welfare. A good way of fostering openness is to undertake a school survey of children, staff and parents. This provides a vehicle for mapping the problem but also engaging all parts of the school community in considering how best to tackle it.

Children in this study indicate that whatever policies and practices are developed to combat bullying, they want to be involved in developing them and in having a say over what action should be taken when they are bullied.

The act of telling about bullying should not be an end in itself, rather, the beginning of a process of unravelling the facts and experiences of the children involved and looking at their needs before deciding **with** the child what is to be done. Some problems of bullying may need to be tackled in a variety of ways before the issue is resolved.

Many children using the ChildLine Bullying Line were in need of emotional support and an opportunity to discuss ways of coping with their own feelings and responding to the behaviour of others. Those children who rang about being bullies had similar needs. The importance of attending to the emotional needs of children is all too frequently underestimated, as is shown by those who said of the Bullying Line: Do you just listen or do you do anything about it? Children tell us they need action - but action appropriate to their individual situation - **and** emotional support.

Adults must support children in exploring their emotional response to being bullied or bullying others; this not only allows children to talk about their feelings and concerns but leads to a discussion of practical solutions which children can influence. If the emphasis is on developing a partnership between the children and adults concerned, then children can be given every opportunity to participate in discussions, make statements about what they would like to happen, and become involved in actions where appropriate. This approach encourages children who have felt powerless and passive to be active on their own behalf, in itself a contribution to developing their self-esteem.

The central role in the response to bullying problems is played by the staff who have responsibility for their care - teachers, play helpers, dinner staff, and care staff for those children living away from home. Many need guidance and training. Some require time and resources, and some the will to take it on. The provision of a defined policy and process, within schools and institutions, for responding to reports of bullying can do much to support and motivate staff. ChildLine experience in working with children in care leads us to believe it is a matter of urgency to translate the development work undertaken in schools into whole-organisation policies for children's homes, secure units and young offenders' institutions.

Policies on their own do make a difference but are not enough. There has to be the will to keep persisting. The clear expectation that it be part of every teacher's and carer's responsibility should permeate guidance for teachers and care staff. But they cannot be left with the sole responsibility, especially if they are untrained, under-resourced, or working in areas where violent street cultures infringe upon school or institutional life. Much more thought and effort also need to go into making the streets and play spaces safe for children. And that is a challenge for all adults. Recent action research published by the Police Research Group (Pitts and Smith, 1995) suggests that anti-bullying programmes are very productive in reducing bullying in schools, though some schools may be more resistant to change than others, particularly where community divisions and racism are enmeshed with the school culture.

Where headteachers and staff are clear about bullying and see the importance of controlling it, have a commitment to educational values and consistent patterns of school and homework, and an attitude to discipline which favours rewards for good behaviour rather than a reliance on punishment, much can be achieved even in the most inauspicious settings. However, it is also time for the Department For Education, alongside education authorities, to identify schools requiring special assistance to reduce violence within them and to offer resources for the establishment of appropriate programmes.

Children ringing ChildLine tell us that adults, teachers and parents bully too. Adults have to be prepared to take responsibility for complaining to colleagues or partners about bullying behaviour. Nothing is more important than this for those especially vulnerable children with communication difficulties which prevent them from drawing attention to the cause of their distress. Adults ought not to maintain a closed shop against children.

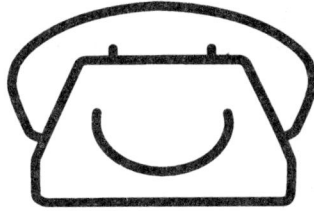

Helping: words into action

The suggestions put forward in this section are to enable adults to help children and young people who are involved in bullying. The good news is that there are lots of ways of tackling bullying, not just one way, (we end this section with a list of resources which describe techniques and strategies); the important thing is to find the right way for each child.

The first step is for children to tell someone about it, their parents, family, friends, a teacher or an older pupil at school; or for an adult to notice that a child is unhappy and consider whether being bullied or bullying might be the reason. Once children can get it off their chests and can say how really awful it makes them feel, then the adult can begin planning alongside them how to get it stopped.

This is usually the teacher's business as well as the child's. Getting the young people concerned round a table and talking about it can make other children see things differently and can challenge the bully's power without fear, fighting or resorting to revenge. Sometimes bullying behaviour is so severe that more serious action has to be taken by parents, headteachers and police. Some bullying is very persistent and difficult to unravel; it can take time to sort out.

The main messages to children are:

- **Don't put up with it**
- **Don't give up**

- Do tell someone who can help
- Do ask them to talk through with you what they plan to do about it before they do anything.

The messages to parents are:

- Do think of bullying if your children seem unhappy or upset.
- Don't wait for children to say they are being bullied before you talk about bullying; children worry more about being bullied than anything else so talk to them about it.
- Do take children seriously if they complain.
- Don't discuss verbal bullying as 'only teasing'.
- Do the obvious - say you love and care for them and tell them they are brave to tell.
- Do talk to them about what is the best course of action; they will have important things to say about what they think is best. Although it is perfectly natural to be furiously angry on your child's behalf and to want to call the bullies to account, it is not the time to let feelings affect judgment.
- Do let the school know that you expect them to discuss with you and your child what they plan to do to put a stop to the bullying, and to be kept informed about what has been done and the outcome.
- Do keep at it - bullying can be hard to stop.
- Do think of things your child can enjoy doing outside of the school and its stresses.
- Do consider whether your child needs to talk to someone else to get help with their confidence and self-esteem.
- Do try to help your child make other friendships.
- Do complain to the school if the problem persists, and write formally if this does not work.

The questions to school and care staff are:

- Do you have a whole school anti-bullying approach in your school or children's home?
- Do you have a specific staff member responsible for

overseeing and developing anti-bullying work?

- **Have you mapped the scale, extent and location of bullying in your school or home through a questionnaire?**
- **Is the anti-bullying literature off the shelf and used effectively?**
- **Are any members of staff in your school or home trained in group approaches?**
- **What curricular work focuses on bullying?**
- **Are children in your school/home directly involved in helping to prevent and stop bullying?**
- **Are non-teaching staff offered training in preventing bullying in the playground?**

While tackling individual incidents of bullying to ensure children's safety is essential, as too is offering emotional support to affected children, schools will not make headway against bullying without a broad strategy for the entire school environment, the so-called 'whole school approach'. **Every school should be doing work to reduce bullying so if yours is not, then why not get a group together and start a campaign?**

Working in partnership

The main message from children to those who wish to help is that any attempt to deal with bullying must include the views and feelings of the children or young people concerned at all stages of the process. Their suggestions should be actively sought, discussed, and acted upon where possible. But children and young people cannot 'go it alone'. They do need effective help from adults to stop bullying. **This means adults and children working in partnership.** Children then become active in resisting the bullying, rather than passive victims, and this in itself can help to increase their self-confidence and sense of self-respect, both likely casualties of the bullying incidents.

Partnership against bullying is necessary in all parts of the effort to reduce violence in schools: prevention; discovering the extent of bullying; establishing a 'zero tolerance' culture; tackling individual incidents; helping bullied and bullying children.

Prevention

Bullying happens in a social context, whether at school, at home, in the street or elsewhere. A key factor is **opportunity** - individuals or groups of children having the opportunity to exert power over another. A second is **means** - children having the means to hurt through physical attack, name-calling or teasing. Therefore minimising opportunity and creating a culture of "no bullying" are the core objectives in tackling bullying.

There are a number of facets to prevention, all fully documented and described in the twin volumes produced from the Sheffield study: Sharp and Smith: *Tackling Bullying in Your School* and Smith and Sharp: *School Bullying*. To summarise, they are:

- **Establishing the scale and extent of the problem through anonymous questionnaire surveys**
- **Supervision suitable to the school environment, the hazard spots, the age of children, and the authority, skill or 'street-cred' of those in charge;**
- **Putting together a working anti-bullying/behaviour policy with clear expectations, rules and sanctions;**
- **Applying the rules without favour or fear of intimidation, fairly and consistently;**
- **Disapproval of verbal abuse on grounds of race, sex or disability;**
- **Adults in schools behaving in ways which children can respect and model;**
- **Education about bullying for children, teachers and parents;**
- **Improving group behaviour through standard groupwork techniques used for team building, and those for handling anger, envy and dislike;**
- **Managing transitions and change with due attention to the**

impact of change and uncertainty on groups;

- **Organising artistic/creative/game/sport activities, which offer children occupation and expression.**

Bringing it into the open

Discovering what and how much bullying is going on is, in itself, a major step towards improving the climate in school. The more bullying is denied, the more it can thrive. This is where partnership between children and adults can be usefully established. Joint management of a programme to establish the extent of the problem and what might help, through a thought- out approach, with various stages to be accomplished and with built-in feedback, is not only an effective approach but also can be part of the curriculum for maths and science.

Tutor groups and class groups, school council, staff, parent and governors' meetings can all address whether the school is safe enough for all its children. A project committee can be established to collate the results of 'Does it happen here?' anonymous questionnaires or discussions, and then short and long-term solutions can be mooted: having safe, quiet/unhappy time/spaces; peer responsibilities for taking care of hurt children; 'first-aid' and first-aiders; guidelines for dealing with individual incidents.

A no-bullying culture

Much will have gone into setting up a no-bullying culture if steps one and two above are undertaken. Cultural change in organisations takes time to achieve and happens through indirect as well as direct action on bullying. Adults' behaviour towards children has an important part to play in this.

ChildLine's first Bullying Report, *Bullying - the Child's View* and the current study revealed that adults' views may be very different from those of children and young people. This being so, part of the project will be a comparison of adults' and children's views and perceptions.

Quite simple means can be used to establish dialogue between adults and children: a flipchart, or white/blackboard for comparing all views is a useful way to tackle different views and opinions. For example, a group of young people in class can write down their experiences of bullying and this can be shown to parents, other teachers, governors, who then can write their own views and reactions alongside the young people's comments. Dialogue and discussion help enormously in attempts to organise and underwrite cultural change.

Handling incidents and complaints

As the case study in schools showed, where schools are actively interested in tackling bullying, many incidents can be dealt with quickly, effectively and with minimal fuss. Teachers and school staff helping children to patch up differences and pointing out hurtful behaviour is, in these schools, routine; and tackling problems early means that fewer serious incidents occur.

Despite this, some children can be afflicted by incidents which are not readily resolved. Each school needs to have a **framework** for tackling these. It is always important to assess each situation in considering what action to take to stop bullying, taking the welfare, feelings and views of children and young people as the starting-point. The framework, like any problem-solving scheme, will have stages: getting the facts; discussing the options; agreeing action; doing what has been agreed; reporting back and follow-up.

Different types and levels of bullying require different responses; so there will be a range of possibilities which vary according to the seriousness of the situation. Is the young person in **immediate danger** from bullies, attackers? Or are they in danger from themselves, have they had suicidal thoughts or made suicide attempts? If the answer is yes, immediate action, to protect the child through emergency referral to medical services, police or social services, may be required.

If no immediate danger exists, or when the danger has been dealt with, a range of possible actions can be explored with children and young people taken from a repertoire of responses: peer counselling/mediation/ monitoring; teacher-led interventions: 'no blame' and 'method of shared concern'; individual discussions; systems of reward for giving up persecuting other children, and sanctions for bullying behaviour; and help from the wider community.

The 'no blame' approach and the 'method of shared concern' are similar in conception. They aim to tackle group bullying in a non-confrontational way, led by a teacher who talks to the children involved either individually or in a group, presenting them with a problem - that one child is unhappy and feeling bullied - and asking those involved (as bystanders or bullies) to help solve the problem. The discussions are problem focused and aim to end with all the pupils agreeing to help improve the situation in some way which they themselves identify. The methods differ in the process and 'scripts' used; emphasis is placed on following the recommended structure closely to ensure a positive outcome.

Peer counselling and mediation schemes have been used in primary and secondary schools where selected children have been trained in basic counselling or mediation skills and identified as sources of help for bullied children or children in dispute with each other. All these techniques are fully described in *Tackling Bullying in Schools* (Sharp, S and Smith, PK, 1995).

The particular approach taken to each incident will depend on a judgment about what precisely is occurring. Is this the persecution of an individual child? Are a group of children being nasty and thoughtless? Is it organised by a troubled child requiring control and help? Is one child feeling angry, envious or jealous of another? Is it caused by disruption or change in a group? Is it linked to family problems? Is this an example of racial, sexual or other discrimination? Is it a signal that a class group requires control and better management and tuition? Such a judgment is made on the basis of information.

Assembling the facts

Teachers will know only too well that establishing what happened can be extremely difficult. Many interventions fail at this point because staff feel they can never get to the bottom of what has really happened. The beauty of the groupwork methods is that their success does not rely on finding out the truth of the matter since they start from the premise that someone is unhappy and upset over something and pose the question "How can we help?" rather than "Who is to blame?"

However, recording of facts from as many sources as possible, including children who are being bullied, bullies, bystanders, parents and other adults, can be a crucial part of any attempt to tackle **persistent** bullying. The facts should include all incidents, whether in or out of school, at the weekend or holidays, as well as in school hours. Different suggestions on how to record appear in the literature on bullying. Again, the more straightforward the problem, the simpler the solution.

Keeping a diary or written record of events has proved a popular and helpful way for children and young people to record what is happening to them. It helps them to feel that they are resisting the bullying and enables them to tell their story.

Records from bystanders - those not directly involved with bullying - as well as people outside the school environment (parents and other adults) provide essential information about the wider context of the lives of children and young people. A practical suggestion is that teachers, or other adults, work with groups of children using paper and pen or a white blackboard. Some children cannot easily use written forms and tape and video recordings will be possibilities for them.

In some cases, the level of bullying or the child's individual circumstances (disablement, for example) are such that more formal processes are required involving social workers, psychologists, psychiatrists, police, governors, and the education authority, where a clear record of the facts can make a great difference to the response child and family receive. A simple **written summary**

highlighting the main points, especially the sequence by date and
time, will enable people in authority, as well as young people
themselves, to review more objectively what is happening and what
can be done to stop the bullying. **Updates and changes** can be
added to the original statements as planning and action develop.
Simple **formats for information gathering and action** are shown
below. A record of action, by whom and with a timespan, is also
helpful, particularly in difficult cases.

(i) Information gathering

Bullied	Bullies	Bystander	Adults trying to help

(ii) Action

Action	By whom	When	Report back review

Discussing the options, planning action, doing what is agreed

Calling a meeting at school, home or on neutral territory is often a successful first step. There information can be shared in as calm an atmosphere as possible and suggestions made about how things can be improved. Including children and young people from the beginning is important in setting up meetings, as is avoiding an atmosphere of blame.

It seems so obvious as to be unnecessary to say that the convenor needs to talk with children and young people about what action will be taken, to include them in the planning process and to check their views regularly as the process develops; but this rarely happens according to the children ringing ChildLine.

Meetings may be very low key - teachers talking with young people - or much more formal and more serious, for example, meeting with police or a child protection case conference. **Children and young people should be involved in all meetings**, wherever they take place. Peer mediation schemes have found that children can convene meetings themselves very effectively.

The meeting agrees what action is to be taken. Like any process of negotiation, it starts with the hope of a straightforward negotiated settlement; more compulsion and supervision will have to happen if negotiation fails. Teachers, playground and lunch-time supervisors must take responsibility for observing the conduct of children thereafter.

Children in our study describe bullying others as a habit they get into. Habits are by definition hard to give up. As one eminent psychiatrist has said: what do they do instead? Some attention needs to be paid to finding other preoccupations.

Reporting back and follow-up

If we have learned anything about bullying at ChildLine it is how persistent it can be. Again and again children call us and say, *"It got better for a time but now it's started again."* Sadly children find that adults get tired of hearing the same story and can easily begin to see the child as a 'whiner' rather than a child in trouble. Children and young people have told ChildLine that even when bullying is stopped and things appear to be going well, follow-up is essential to keep bullying at bay.

In order then to make action effective, it must be monitored, and a record made of the main conclusions and planned action. Written copies of the main points of the meeting should be given to everybody who attends. Follow-up meetings to review what is happening can be set at the time of the meeting - this can be a plan to meet within the next hour, day, weeks or months. Children and young people should be given the opportunity to ask for a meeting when they feel one is necessary and not told, "We don't think it's necessary now because everything is alright."

Giving up on negotiation

There may come a time when the realistic decision is to give up on trying to improve the situation by negotiation. It can help children to understand the seriousness of persecution to have police talk to them, and, in some cases, to caution or lay a charge. Children should not have to put up with being assaulted.

Sometimes the bullying child or children will have to be excluded from school. Assessments of individual children by professionals such as psychologists, medical professionals, social workers, are important if the underlying factors which may be contributing toward bullying are to be understood and dealt with effectively. Exclusion or expulsion need to be accompanied by treatment; for research clearly identifies persistent bullying behaviour with later criminality (Olweus). Sometimes the only solution is for the child to move school, though this is not always possible in areas served by only one school. ChildLine has heard from parents who have felt forced to move home to help their child escape bullying. Some children find that bullying begins again at the new school. But we have heard from parents and children who have found that this **has** made the difference and allowed the child to begin again in a new environment, free of history.

Helping children recover

Alongside action to put a stop to the bullying must go attention to the child's emotional state. The children ringing ChildLine are eloquent in describing the level of fear, disablement, and anguish they experience. Children involved in bullying, whether bullied, bystanders or bullies, may need ongoing help for some period of time to resolve the emotional impact of bullying and/or difficulties within the family, school or the individual. Anxieties, fear, and the effect of being bullied, do not quickly disappear.

We have referred to the importance of offering love, comfort and support to the suffering child and of finding ways of increasing self-esteem and self-confidence. Talking to a trusted adult in confidence, whether at home, school or, for example, ChildLine, may also be necessary. The decision to use help or counselling should on the whole be made by the child or young person themselves; but adults can help by telling the young people where to go to get help and by offering encouragement.

ChildLine has learned a great deal in nine years about counselling children and young people and giving them emotional support. The process involved can be described as follows.

1. To stop and listen to what the child and young person is saying and to check out with them if your understanding, as an adult, is the same as their's. This may take a few minutes or may take several hours/sessions over a period of time.

2. To allow the young person time and space to describe their anxieties and fears about the results of telling and not telling, and also the likely consequences of any planned action.

3. To ask the young person for their suggestions about what can be done and to agree with them a joint plan of action.

Children experiencing the **long-term effects of bullying**, such as low self-esteem, inability to go to school, to get on with school work or to make successful relationships with their peers may require intensive counselling with a 'confidential person' long after the bullying has stopped. Bullying lasting only a brief period may still have effects months or years later.

Counselling is in many ways a grandiose term for an activity which is at its best simple in form, though not simple to perform. It means giving someone your full attention, listening to what they are saying and not saying, encouraging them to face the worst about themselves and others and to recognise good experiences; to put into words, pictures, thoughts or feelings what requires to be expressed, thinking about what an experience means for the present and the future, and helping them to change what they feel and what they do, if these are troubling to themselves and others.

Some young people get enough comfort and support from one conversation; others may need many or other forms of help. This kind of help can be offered by other children who are befrienders, by teachers, parents or relatives. But sometimes children prefer private, confidential help from somewhere like ChildLine or a school counsellor.

Referral to psychologists, social workers, counsellors, therapists, can be offered to the young person at any stage in the process, but it may not be until a review meeting, or a follow-up discussion, weeks or months later that the need for continuing, specialised, emotional support becomes clear.

From ChildLine's research, it is also clear that adults need help and support themselves in order to help children with bullying. Some of the most effective support has been from parents' groups which have been involved in trying to tackle bullying in a particular school or community. These are particularly effective if they work alongside teachers, governors and young people who are closely involved in anti- bullying programmes. Those without support should actively seek out other parents and adults and possibly professionals, for example educational psychologists, who can be a reference point and support for them as they attempt to help children and young people involved in bullying.

Helping children stop themselves bullying

Many parents are horrified to find out that their children have bullied others. It would really be much easier if we all expected our children to behave nastily from time to time. ChildLine's training workshop for counsellors on bullying asks everyone to think of when they were last bullied and when they last bullied someone else. Like adults, most children will exert power unreasonably at some time or enjoy behaving unpleasantly, even maliciously, to someone else. If they are offered every encouragement to do this from friends, family and colleagues, they may go further than they could ever imagine in behaving wrongly to others. This is not to deny that some young people are motivated by quite sadistic feelings and have little conscience or sense of wrongdoing to hold them back, just as some adults do.

There is no simple prescription to fit every case. The approach to be taken depends again on how the behaviour is understood to have occurred: is it taking out bad feelings on others? simple envy? scapegoating as part of a group? expressing firm feelings of dislike and hatred? deep-seated feelings of anger which are uncontrolled? thoughtless nastiness? a symptom of individual or family disturbance? or malevolence?

Non-punitive approaches like the no-blame approach allow children to change their behaviour without feeling so bad about themselves that they have even more bad feelings to take out on others. But some children require more active control and others require a clear sense that this bullying behaviour is not going to pay and that better behaviour will. Yet others will need individual and counselling help. Good detection in itself is an effective deterrent. All children benefit from seeing that children who bully don't get away with it.

Resources and further information

Much excellent work has been published in recent years about counteracting bullying. The following are a selection of the resources available. This wealth of material means that adults really have no excuse for allowing bullying to persist.

FOR HELP AND ADVICE CONTACT:

ChildLine
2nd Floor
Royal Mail Building
Studd Street
London N1 0QW.
*Any child or young person can call ChildLine at any time about any problem
on 0800 1111. The call is free. Because of the huge demand for the service,
it can sometimes be difficult to get through, but do keep trying. If children
prefer they can write to ChildLine at: ChildLine, Freepost 1111, London
N1 0BR. No stamp is needed.*

Advisory Centre for Education (ACE)
1b Aberdeen Studios
22 Highbury Grove
London N5 2EA.
0171-354 8321
*Telephone advice lines mainly for parents, teachers and governors. Open on
weekdays from 2.00 to 5.00 p.m. ACE also publishes information sheets and
handbooks. Relevant ACE publications include:*

Governors and Bullying	*£1.00*
Governors and Discipline	*£1.00*
Taking Matters Further	*£1.00*
Special Education Handbook	*£7.50*
Bullying: Advice for Parents	*£1.00*

Kidscape,
152 Buckingham Palace Road
London SW1W 9TR.
0171-730 3300
*Telephone helpline for parents and schools. Open Monday and Wednesday
9.30 to 5.00 p.m. For information sheets and publications list send large
s.a.e.*

The Scottish Council for Research in Education (SCRE)
15 St John Street
Edinburgh EH8 8JR
Bullying and How to Fight it - A guide for Families £3.25

Anti-bullying Campaign
10 Borough High Street
London SE1 9QQ
0171-378 1446
Telephone advice line open Monday to Friday 9.30 to 5.30 p.m.
(Answerphone when lines closed)

Children's Legal Centre,
Colchester 01206 872561
Advice line available Monday to Friday 2.00 to 5.00 p.m.

The Samaritans
See local telephone directory for numbers. Free confidential helpline for anyone suffering distress

Education Otherwise,
P.O. Box 120
Leamington Spa
Warwicks CV32 7ER
01926 886828

A self-help organisation offering support, advice and information to families practising or thinking about home education. Publication list available. Publishes School is not Compulsory.

Education Law Association (ELAS)
Lawn Cottage
Lodge Lane
Salfords
Surrey RH1 5DH.

Can give names and addresses of solicitors throughout the country who specialise in education law.

Literature

Bennett, N. and **Dunne, E.** (1992)
Managing classroom groups.
Hemel Hempstead: Simon and Schuster

Cowie, H. and **Pecherek, A.** (1994)
Counselling: Approaches and issues in Education.
London: David Fulton

Cowie, H. and **Sharp, S.** (1994)
Tackling Bullying in your school.
London: Routledge

DFE (1994)
Bullying - don't suffer in silence. An anti- bullying pack for schools.
HMSO

Elliott, M.(ed) (1991)
Bullying: A practical guide to coping for schools.
Harlow: Longman

Fisher, R. and **Ury, W.** (1990)
Getting to yes, negotiating agreement without giving in. London:
Hutchinson

Howe, F. and **Tuthill, J.** (1994)
Tackling Bullying.
NSPCC

Johnstone, M. Munn, P and **Edwards, L.** (1991)
Action against bullying: A support pack for schools.
Edinburgh: SCRE

Kidscape (1990)
Bully Courts. Kidscape,
152 Buckingham Palace Road, London SW1W 9TR

Kidscape (1993)
Stop Bullying. Kidscape,
152 Buckingham Palace Road, London SW1W 9TR

La Fontaine, J. 1991
Bullying: The child's view.
London: Calouste Gulbenkian Foundation

Maines, B and **Robinson, G.** (1992)
Michael's story: The 'no-blame approach'.
Lame Duck Publishing, 10 South Terrace,
Redlands, Bristol B56 6TG

Mellor, A. (1993)
Bullying and how to fight it: A guide for families.
Edinburgh: SCRE

Munn, P. (1993)
School action against bullying: Involving parents and non-teaching staff.
Edinburgh: SCRE

Pikas, A. (1989)
A pure concept of mobbing gives the best results for treatment.
School Psychology International 10, p95-104

Olweus, D. (1993b)
Bullying in schools: What we know and what we can do.
Oxford: Blackwell

S. Sharp and **P.K. Smith** (eds)
Tackling bullying in your school: A practical handbook for teachers.
London: Routledge

Skinner, A. (1992)
Bullying: an annotated bibliography of literature and resources.
Youth Work Press, 17-23 Albion Street, Leicester LE1 6GD

Smith, P.K. and **Sharp, S.** (1994)
School Bullying.
Routledge

Rosemary Stones (1993)
Don't pick on me: How to handle bullying.
Piccadilly Press Ltd, 5 Castle Road, London NW1 8PR

Tattum, D.P. (ed) (1993)
Understanding and managing bullying.
London: Heinemann

Tattum, D.P. and **Herbert, G.** (1993)
Countering bullying.
Stoke- on-Trent: Trentham Books

Bibliography

ACE Bulletin 34, 6-11 (1990)
Governors and bullying

Bennett, N. and **Dunne, E.** (1992)
Managing classroom groups.
Hemel Hempstead: Simon and Schuster

Besag, V. (1989)
Bullies and victims in schools.
Milton Keynes: Open University Press

Bion, W. R. (1961)
Experiences in Groups.
London: Tavistock Publications.

Blatchford, P. (1989)
Playtime in the primary school. Problems and improvements.
Windsor: NFER-Nelson

Boal, A. (1979)
Theatre of the oppressed.
London: Pluto Press

Cowie, H. (October 1995)
Approaches to Peer Counselling.
Young Minds Newsletter Issue 23

Cowie, H. and **Pecherek, A.** (1994)
Counselling: Approaches and issues in Education.
London: David Fulton

Cowie, H. and **Sharp, S.** (1994)
Tackling Bullying in your school.
London: Routledge

Department of Education and Science (1989)
Discipline in schools: Report of the committee chaired by Lord Elton.
London: HMSO

DFE (1994)
Bullying - don't suffer in silence. An anti- bullying pack for schools.
HMSO

Elliott, M.(ed) (1991)
Bullying: A practical guide to coping for schools.
Harlow: Longman

Farrington, D.P. (1993)
Understanding and preventing bullying. In **M. Tonry** and **N. Morris**
(eds), *Crime and justice: An annual review of research,* vol. 17.
p.399.
Chicago: University of Chicago Press.

Fisher, R. and **Ury, W.** (1990)
Getting to yes, negotiating agreement without giving in.
London: Hutchinson

Gulbenkian Foundation (1993)
*One scandal too many .. the case for comprehensive protection for children
in all settings.*

Howe, F. and **Tuthill, J.** (1994)
Tackling Bullying.
NSPCC

Johnstone, M. Munn, P and **Edwards, L.** (1991)
Action against bullying: A support pack for schools.
Edinburgh: SCRE

Keighram, K. and **Houghton, A.** (Sept 1994)
Tayside Region Bullying Helpline - The First Five Months

Kelly, E. and **Cohn, T.** (1988)
Racism in schools: New research evidence.
Stoke-on-Trent: Trentham Books

Kidscape (1990)
Bully Courts.
Kidscape, 152 Buckingham Palace Road, London SW1W 9TR

Kidscape (1993)
Stop Bullying. Kidscape, 152 Buckingham Palace Road, London
SW1W 9TR

La Fontaine, J. 1991
Bullying: The child's view.
London: Calouste Gulbenkian Foundation

Maines, B and **Robinson G.** (1992)
Michael's story: The 'no-blame approach'.
Lame Duck Publishing, 10 South Terrace, Redlands, Bristol B56
6TG

Mellor, A. (1991) Helping victims. In **M. Elliott** (ed),
Bullying: A practical guide to coping for schools.
Harlow: Longman

Mellor, A. (1993)
Bullying and how to fight it: A guide for families.
Edinburgh: SCRE

Munn, P. (1993)
School action against bullying: Involving parents and non-teaching staff.
Edinburgh: SCRE

Olweus, D. (1993b)
Bullying in schools: What we know and what we can do.
Oxford: Blackwell

Pikas, A. (1989)
A pure concept of mobbing gives the best results for treatment.
School Psychology International 10, pp95-104

Pitts, John and **Smith, Philip,** (1996) Police Research Group
report *Preventing School Bullying.*
PRG, Room 448, Home Office,
50 Queen Anne's Gate, London SW1H 9AT

Russell, D.E.H. (1983)
The incidence and prevalence of intrafamilial and extrafamilial sexual abuse of female children,
Child Abuse and Neglect 7, pp133-146.

Sharp, S and **Smith, P. K.**(eds)
Tackling bullying in your school: A practical handbook for teachers.
London: Routledge

Skinner, A. (1992)
Bullying: an annotated bibliography of literature and resources.
Youth Work Press, 17-23 Albion Street, Leicester LE1 6GD

Smith, P.K. and **Sharp, S.** (1994)
School Bullying.
Routledge

Rosemary Stones (1993)
Don't pick on me: How to handle bullying.
Piccadilly Press Ltd, 5 Castle Road, London NW1 8PR

Tattum, D.P. (ed) (1993)
Understanding and managing bullying.
London: Heinemann

Tattum, D.P. and **Herbert, G.** (1993)
Countering bullying.
Stoke- on-Trent: Trentham Books

Tower Hamlets Education Department (John Sinnott - 0171 364
4942) *Living in Tower Hamlets: a survey of the attitudes of secondary
school pupils*

Trust for the Study of Adolescence (1995)
Teenage Suicide and Self-harm.
TSA Publishing